THE BRIGHTON BOYS SERIES

BY

LIEUTENANT JAMES R. DRISCOLL

AS FOLLOWS:

It was a Race for a few Seconds

The BRIGHTON BOYS at CHATEAU-THIERRY

BY
LIEUTENANT JAMES R. DRISCOLL

———

ILLUSTRATED

———

THE JOHN C. WINSTON COMPANY
PHILADELPHIA

CONTENTS

ILLUSTRATIONS

The Brighton Boys at Chateau Thierry

CHAPTER I

OVERHEARD

"YOU'RE just plain scared, I guess."
"You're just plain wrong. Anyway,
people in glass shanties shouldn't
throw rocks. I don't see you trying to play
soldier." The last speaker, a tall lad who
sat nearest the window in the rear seat of a
crowded railroad car seemed exasperated by
the uncomplimentary suggestion of the boy
beside him, a short, heavy-set, curly-headed
fellow, who looked even more youthful than
his sixteen years. His handsome face lighted
up with a smile when he spoke; evidently
there was but little enmity back of his teasing.

"If I were a telegraph pole and had your
gray hairs, Stapley, you can bet your number
nines I'd be in camp. But they won't take
kids."

"That's right, Richards; they won't, unless a fellow's dad signs his consent. My dad won't do it. So kindly apologize, will you? My gray hairs deserve it; I'm a year older than you are, you know. Go on; I'm listening."

"Come off! Anybody can coax his governor not to sign. Honest, now; don't you like the idea of getting a bullet—?"

"Now cut that out. You think you're some kidder, but it takes an expert to kid me. Of course I know you're sore over the lambasting we gave your team at basket ball. All Brighton is laughing about it yet."

"Never get cross over accidents. Couldn't help it if Terry wasn't fit. How about the game before that and the score? Eh?" Richards' smile broadened.

"Well, was I sore?" Stapley challenged.

"Like a hen after a bath. You couldn't see anything but red. The same at the class relay runs and—"

"I'd hate to say that you and the truth are total strangers," Stapley said, quickly.

"Oh, let her go. I consider the source, as the man said when the donkey kicked him, 'The critter didn't know any bet—.' Now, what's the matter?"

The boy by the window had suddenly made a sudden downward motion with one hand and held a finger of the other to his lips, looking most mysterious. He had previously chanced to lean far forward, a position which he now maintained for a moment; then he flopped down against the seat back, quickly taking a pencil and a scrap of paper from his pocket and beginning to write. In another minute Richards was scanning what had been written:

"You know German. So do I—a little, but Dad made me take Spanish this term. I just caught a word or two from those dubs ahead that sounded funny. You cock your ear over the back of the seat and listen some. If you let on you're mad as blazes at me and now and then give me a bawling out, I'll play dumb and then when you wait for me to reply maybe you can hear a thing or two they're saying. We've got to bury the hatchet now, for we are both Americans, first."

The younger lad at once did as requested, glancing at the two men in the seat ahead, who were in earnest conversation, one, evidently under some excitement, talking quite loudly. He seemed not to think his voice carried so far above the rumble of a railroad train, or else they both considered as naught the chance that anyone might understand the language they were speaking. That the two were foreigners there could be no doubt; the full whiskered face of one, and the bent, thin lips of the other denoted, beyond power of words, the egotistical, would-be-dominating Prussian blood. It was an argument over ways and means that caused the bearded fellow to become so vehement.

The lad, understanding conversational German fairly well because of his persistent practice at school and the influence of a nurse he had when small, caught at first but a few words from the whiskered foreigner; then, when the smooth-faced man began speaking at length in a voice that could not be plainly heard the boy quickly carried out the suggestion of his companion.

Donald Richards took real enjoyment in doing this, and to Clement Stapley it was an ordeal to accept it without showing more than a grimace of protest. The two lads had long been far from friendly. They hailed from the same town, Lofton, perched well up in the foothills of the Red Deer Mountains, and they had ever been rivals, since early boyhood, in games, contests of skill, popularity among their fellows. Clement was the only child of the great man of the town, the senior Stapley being president of mills that made the place a spot of some importance on the map. Donald was one of five sons of the leading physician in the town and, having to paddle his own canoe against a more active competition, he had naturally become more self-reliant and shrewd than the half-spoiled son of the rich man.

When the two entered Brighton they were not admitted to the same classes, for Don had advanced beyond Clem in learning, even though younger, but they engaged in contests of skill and strength, and both become partial leaders of *cliques* such as naturally form within classes, and possessed the *esprit de corps* that is always uppermost among youths. Clem, tall and manly, with a dignity of manner and the prestige of his father's wealth and standing back of him, drew a certain crowd of followers in the institution, while Don, active in both brain and muscle far beyond his years and possessing a born air of leadership, had admirers everywhere. Naturally, as with the analytical minds of youths being trained to compare and classify, the relative merits of the two boys were weighed and counted in such a

manner as to wave still harder the red flag
of bitter competition until never a kind word
passed between them, but always *repartee*,
often with rancor, once or twice in such anger
that they almost came to blows.

Now, in the Christmas holidays of 1917–18,
the students of old Brighton, one and all,
were departing for their homes. Chancing
to go a little late, Don and Clem found
themselves in the same train with but one
unoccupied seat and at once the old-time
banter began, with a question from Don
relative to a subject uppermost in the minds
of the youth of the United States: Was
Clem going to enlist, and if not, why not?
If the interruption occasioned by the two
men in front of the boys had not occurred,
there might have been another serious
quarrel.

CHAPTER II

TRACED

D ON'S face was a study as he suddenly left off berating his companion and listened quite breathlessly to the rising inflections of the bearded man making answer to his hatchet-faced companion. The boy was hearing something interesting; that Clem knew, and he waited with some impatience to find out what it might be. After awhile the two men in front began to exchange words much too rapidly for Don to get a clear idea what they were driving at. Presently one of them turned suddenly and gave the lad a searching, suspicious glance; then with another word in a low tone the two stopped talking. Don maintained his position of leaning forward, his face at the back of the seat ahead for a few minutes, at the same time unmercifully badgering Clem until the men both turned to see what it was all about and to put them at ease Don laughed and made a motion with his head toward his companion, as much as to say he would welcome an audience. This must have reassured the men a little, though the hatchet-faced fellow turned quickly and fired a German sentence at the boy. Don was not to be caught by such a trick; he looked blank and shook his head.

"You'll have to say that in United States, mister," he laughed. The German turned away, and the two began talking again in so low a tone that the words were inaudible, especially as at that moment the train started to glide over newly ballasted tracks and the rumble was increased. So the two left their seat and walked back in the car where they got their heads together.

"Sounds like funny stuff," Don said hurriedly. They're up to something queer. Whiskers' said there'd be enough to blow things to pieces; that's all I made out. They seemed to mean some building, but I couldn't quite catch what."

"Great snakes! They're a couple of dyna-miters!" Clem declared.

"Don't know, but it looks like it. I have a hunch they're going to destroy something or other."

"Where?"

"I couldn't make out. Don't think they said where. That was understood."

"When?"

"Couldn't tell that, either."

"What else did you get?"

"Not much; nothing. But that's about enough; isn't it?"

"Well, maybe. You know we ought to follow 'em, and see where they get off, and put somebody on to them. It's a duty. Likely they'll change cars at Upgrove for the city."

"Well, even at that we could get back before very late," Don said.

"We don't both have to go. One's enough. We can draw for it can't we?"

"Sure. But we've got to hurry. Lofton's next; about six minutes. Here, let's toss up. What's yours?"

"Heads. Hold on! The ginks are fixing to get off at Lofton, as sure as you're——"

The sentence was not finished. The full-bearded German got up to reach for a bundle in the rack above, and the other man lifted a big satchel from the floor. The men got into the aisle and started for the forward end. Not until they were out on the platform and the train almost at a standstill did the boys slip back and into their overcoats, grab their suit cases and make for the

2

rear end, being careful to drop off on the side away from the station platform and then to dodge quickly around a freight car that stood on the siding, peeping beneath it toward the glimmering lights, for now it had begun to grow dark. It chanced that only these four male passengers and one woman got off at Lofton and there was no one waiting for the train, except the station master; therefore, it became an easy matter to note the movements of the two men.

"They're going out along the track, in a hurry too," Clem said.

"Going to cross—yes, there they go," was Don's observation.

"Out the Galaville road. Come on; let's see where—"

"I'm going to chuck this suit case in the station."

"Here, too. Danny Morgan's got to wait for the up train."

"Turn up your collar and pull down your lid, Clem, so's to show no white."

"And get a move on, Don; those fellows are in a big hurry."

A mutual object quickly brought these lads to a friendly, even familiar understanding, proved by the use of their first names and their quick agreement in action. Both noticed it, but they were either too proud or too much engrossed to refer to it openly. Ahead of them lay an apparently necessary purpose and they followed it with the quick determination that belongs to the well balanced, bright-minded school boy. It could be said of old Brighton that it put self-reliant energy and pep into its pupils; no youngsters anywhere could be prouder of the zeal to do and the encouragement therefor, which spoke volumes for the accomplishments of that student body, and in athletics, as well as for the many graduates who had attained high standing in various fields of endeavor. In nothing was this better shown than by the lads who entered the war and won distinction.

It was no light task to follow those hurrying, distant figures on a darkening winter night, along what soon became a winding, lonely, tree or thicket-lined by-way. The town ended at the station and only one house faced the Galaville road beyond for more than half a mile.

The dim figures could barely be seen far ahead and not wishing to be observed, the boys kept as near as possible to the edge of

the road, along a fence or an overhanging
clay bank on one side. They soon gained on
the men; then, fearing discovery, they fell
back. But even at this they knew that
presently they must be seen; it was natural
that these men should look behind them
and when crossing a knoll the lads could
not avoid showing against the sky. Then
the road began to descend, and the pursued
stopped and stood a moment.

"Keep right on slowly," Don's quicker wits
advised. "They'll smell a mouse if we stop,
too. Come on; they won't know we don't
live out this way."

Again the men, possibly somewhat reassured and yet not wanting to be overtaken,
hurried on and were soon out of sight around
a bend.

"Wonder if they'll sneak into the bushes to
see who we are," Clem queried.

"No; they'll only hurry more so as to
turn off at a road or path," Don argued and
he proved to be right. From the bend the
two figures could barely be discerned. To
hurry after them would excite suspicion, but
now fair chance come to the boys' aid. Just
beyond, and evidently unknown to the
German-speaking pair, a path led across a

meadow that short cut another sharp bend in the road and this enabled Clem and Don to gain so much on the men that before the latter had reached the farm house beyond, the lads were close behind them, between a double line of willow trees and thus unseen.

But here the adventure was to end for the time. The boys, instinctively aware that the men believed they were beyond observation, now were eager to see which road of a fork beyond would be followed and they were not greatly surprised when the travelers turned in at the gate of the farm house and knocked at the door. A light appeared at the entrance, a large figure loomed in the doorway, a few words were exchanged in voluble German; then the door closed.

"They're friends of Shultz, by jimminy!" Clem exploded.

"They are, you bet! That big fat slob of a saloon keeper was in the door," Don added.

"Let's go home. We can look into this further, but later," Clem advised and the boys almost reluctantly retraced their steps.

CHAPTER III

BANG

CHRISTMAS festivities at Lofton, like those in nearly every live town in the United States, were such as to engross the attention of the youthful population, especially the rehearsing for Christmas Eve carols. The plans for home enjoyments, the doing up of packages, procuring and trimming of trees and many other happy duties kept both boys about their widely separated homes very busy.

Clem Stapley lived in the mansion on a hill overlooking the town and the mills. Don Richards dwelt in a big house on the main street. In the days following—the Sunday and Monday preceding Christmas—the lads saw each other but once, and then only to exchange a few words. These had been in effect that if the suspected strangers were up to any mischief here they would probably defer it until after Christmas, and now spend the time having a beer-fest with fat old Shultz. Clem thought more probably that the men had gone away again, or would soon go, but Don believed otherwise; he had been reading of German propaganda and plots against munition factories and ships, and with a mind keen for gathering facts and making deductions, he felt, half instinctively, that there must be an evil purpose in these men stopping in this town where the large factory was turning out war materials for the Government. It was almost with a conscientious protest that he turned now to the immediate business of Christmas gaieties.

And the jolliest day of the year came on with its usual zest and pleasure, and went quickly by. Late in the afternoon Don and a younger brother, to try new skates, went out to the pond not far from the Galaville road and as they were returning, just at dusk, they observed three men standing on a high knoll just above the road and looking off toward the town, one pointing, with outstretched arm, from time to time. The figures could be clearly seen against the sky: one, a short fellow, apparently with whiskers, one a slender, tall chap and the other big, paunchy, heavy-set. It did not require much imagination to identify them as Shultz and his two guests—the Germans of the train.

The boys were evidently not seen. Don commanded his brother to follow him and kept on the far side of a row of cedar trees until they were out of sight of the hill. He found himself much disturbed by the circumstance, trivial as it seemed; and yet, was it trivial? It was possible that these men were merely out for exercise, or a bit of novelty; they may have been simply noting the interesting features of the town, or even contemplating the purchase of farm land near that of Shultz.

That night Don went to bed with the subject still uppermost in his mind to the extent that it was becoming rather tiresome because barren of results; and beyond any chance of solution. More to relieve his mind than anything else he managed to get Clement Stapley on the telephone quite late and told him of seeing the men, half expecting his partner in the mystery to characterize him as a boob for considering such a thing of sufficient importance to bother him. To his surprise Clem appeared tremendously interested and insisted on their getting together the next morning. Don agreed, hung up and went to bed. He usually slept like a log, the result of good health and a clear conscience, he himself declared, and there could be little doubt of this, but however tightly wrapped in the all-absorbing arms of slumber, the dulling influence suddenly and entirely relaxed an hour or so after midnight. Along with a large majority of the townspeople, according to later evidence, he found himself sitting up in bed and wondering why the house was trying to do a dance and the windows to imitate a drum corps. Then came voices from within, some in alarm, others in quieter comment and the words:

"Great fury! Is the house coming down?" from Merrill, next to Don in age.

"What was that, Dad?" a younger scion questioned.

"An explosion of some kind; two of them!" This from the doctor.

"Where 'bouts?"

"Yes, where do you think it was, Father?"

"Over on the other side of town; perhaps the mills."

"Ooh! Can we go an' see, Daddy?" This from the baby of the family.

"No; in the morning. It's only two o'clock now. Go to sleep."

"But you're going, **Father**; they may need you," Donald offered.

"Yes, and I'll take you with me."

It was the mills. One building with the office in part, had been utterly wrecked, another had been partly destroyed and one end was on fire. And while the volunteer department and helpers were valorously extinguishing the flames another explosion occurred that hurt two men and flung some others down, Don amongst them. The boy was uninjured, though the jarring up made him see red. But with a shrewdness beyond his years he kept silent as to what he suspected and his ears were keen to catch the talk going on around him. It seemed to be the idea of one and all that this was the work of German spies.

Presently, from behind some splintered boxes, they found the half-unconscious watchman and resuscitated him, getting him to talk. He had obtained one good look at the miscreants as they ran away.

Don kept an eye open for Clem and as that youth appeared leaping with his father, from a big motor car, he was grabbed and pulled aside.

"Don't say a word about what we know," Don whispered. "Here's a chance for us to get right up on top of everybody. It was those two, Clem."

"But, look here, Don, Father ought to know—"

"Sure! And he will, sooner and more satisfactorily than if he put some of those bum detectives on the job; you know that. They'd kick around for about a week, but you and I can get busy right now; to-night. They won't get here before—"

"But Father can have those men arrested and then—"

"Oh, hang it, yes, and give us the go-by! Let's be the ones to spring the surprise. Come on; I'm ready to tackle it, when I get a gun somewhere."

The idea appealed to Clement Stapley, for he did not want to be outdone in daring by his old-time rival. It would never do for Don to say: "Clem fell down on the job; wasn't equal to it; hadn't the backbone." He turned to Don:

"I'm with you! Hold on, I can fix the shooting-iron matter. Wait half a minute." Into the debris of the office wreck the lad climbed and wriggled, and after a moment's looking about, in the light from the yard lamp-poles, which had been re-established by some quick-witted employee, the boy located a shattered desk, pried open a drawer and drew forth two long-barreled revolvers of the finest make.

Don, waiting and watching, heard Mr. Stapley say to several men:

"I have a notion that those fellows will come back. They'll believe we think they've left for distant parts and that will make them bold. You see they've got reason: the stock mill wasn't hurt. Riley found two bombs that hadn't gone off in there; the fuses had become damp, I suppose. And that was probably the big game they were after. Probably they'll take another chance at it. Well, we'll put detectives on the job as soon as possible. Have any of you noticed anyone about; any strangers whom you could have suspected?"

There was a general negative to this; then one hand spoke up:

"How about that fellow Shultz, out beyond the station? He's a red-hot German and before we went into the war he was shouting pro-Prussian stuff till his throat was sore. He's about the only Hun around here except old man Havemeyer, and he's a decent, good citizen and wants to see the kaiser punched full of holes."

"Yes, Havemeyer is all right," assented Mr. Stapley, "but we will have to look into the doings of this Shultz."

CHAPTER IV

CAPTURED

THE destruction from the explosions was not so damaging but that complete repairs could be made in a few weeks and the work, crowded into the other buildings, go on without serious interruption. Mr. Stapley, organizing a crowd of workers on the spot, turned for one moment to listen to his son.

"Say, Dad, it would be a fine thing to land the dubs that did this; wouldn't it? I have an idea—"

The president of the Stapley Mills laughed outright. "That you know the miscreants? Oh, the confidence and the imagination of youth! Well, go bring them in, my son; bring them right in here!"

"Well, maybe it's only a joke, but—but, Dad, if I did—if we did, would you—?"

"I'd give you about anything you'd ask for if you even got a clue to the devils! What do you know—anything?"

"Tell you later, Dad. Would you—er—let me—enlist?"

"Yes, even that! Anything! But here now, don't you go and start anything rash. Better wait until the detectives and police get on the job. I'm too busy now to—"

"All right. See you later, Dad."

Slipping away in the darkness, the boys began talking in low tones, and made for the Galaville road, laying plans as they went. Don offered the principal suggestions and Clem, lacking definite ideas of proceeding, was fair enough to comply. They approached the Shultz farmhouse with keen caution, making a wide detour and coming from back of the barn. A dog barked near the house and that was the only sign of life. But there was a method of bestirring the inmates, and the boys believed that the miscreants would show themselves to render hasty aid to a fellow countryman in gratitude for the shelter and care they had received from Shultz.

Working like beavers the lads gathered a lot of loose cornstalks, tall straws, and barnyard litter of a most inflammable nature, and piled it all on the side of the barn opposite the house, and far enough away to be beyond danger. At half a dozen places almost at once they set fire to the pile and having selected positions of ambush they rushed

into hiding, Clem behind the barn bridge,
Don crouching in the shadow of the corn-crib.
The signal of action was to be the sudden
move of either.

The plan worked. No one could have
turned in and slept at once after the noise
of the explosion in the town, much less these
people who, the lads felt assured, had been
expecting it. If the farmhouse occupants
had been in fear of showing themselves
they would ignore that for the few minutes
needed for saving the animals in a burning
barn. That they would, on looking out,
believe the barn was on fire there could be
no question, as no view from the house
could detect the exact location of the flames.

A door slammed; there was the sound of
excited words, of commands, of hurrying
feet. Could it be possible that only Shultz
and his family would appear on the scene?
Had the Germans of the train departed?
Or was it, after all, merely a coincidence
that those men had come here and had talked
in the train in a way that led the boys to
think they were up to some such tricks,
and that others had caused the explosion?
Might it not have been some workman who
was a German sympathizer?

Such doubts filled the minds of the young adventurers as they waited, hidden, and wondering. But they were not long to remain in doubt for things began to happen. Fat Shultz was not the first to appear, for three figures rounded the corner of the barn ahead of his puffing form.

The dog was fleetest of foot; that half-mongrel dachshund bade fair to spoil the game for the boys, for he was far more interested in the presence of strangers than in a bonfire, no matter how high it blazed. Yawcub, or whatever the beast was called, began to bark at the corn-crib, but the followers of the elongated hound fortunately paid no attention to this. Close together came the next in line—Fraülein Shultz and a man, both plainly seen as they came within the zone of light from the fire. The woman turned the corner and stopped as though she had bumped against a post, her hands going to her bosom in relief and for want of breath. The man almost ran into her; then he let out a German remark, doubtless an oath, and wheeled about. Surprise number one had relieved, if disgusted, him; number two, which confronted him before he had taken two retracing steps, made him lift his arms as if trained in the art.

"Hands up!" was Don's order.

"And be blamed quick about it!" supplemented Clem.

"And you, too, Shultz!" Don addressed the on-coming and puffing old saloon keeper.

"Eh? Vat? Bah! I safe mein barn! I safe mein horses und coos und mein piks!"

"Hands up and stop! Your horses and cows and pigs are all safe. Put your hands up, if you don't want to get some lead in you!"

Shultz stopped, but rather at the command or announcement of his more active wife than because of an order from his captors. His bumptious self-importance would not permit him to knuckle to anybody, much less to mere American youths.

"Huh! Vat? Chust poys, py gollies! Raus mit 'em! Clear oudt! I ring der necks off bodt! Put down dose pistols! Eh? Vat? Bah!"

It instantly became evident that something most radical, however unpleasant, must be done to convince this egotistical German what young America can do when started. The preparations for war, the flower of our youth enlisting, the early determination to beat the Huns had evidently made little impression on this tub of conceited Prussian-

3

ism. It was the certain duty of his youthful captors to impress not only a lesson on
Shultz, but to maintain their own position
in the *rôle* they had chosen to assume. The
necessity was also very apparent of repelling
a weighty and sudden charge of the declared
enemy, for Shultz, by reason of his calling,
was given to combatting foes of almost
every sort, albeit this must have been a
somewhat new experience.

It was Don who, as usual, saw first the need
of action and improved upon it. Your trained,
competing athlete, boxer, wrestler, leader
of team contests must be as quick with
his head as with his hands and the event of
weapons on a possibly tragic mission and
against a really dangerous opponent flabbergasted the boy not a bit. Words, he saw,
were entirely useless; delay might be fatal—
to someone, at least.

The boy's revolver barked and spit out
its fiery protest over Shultz's head; the
tongue of flame against the dark background
of the night was enough to command any
minion of the Old Scratch, and Shultz proved
no exception to this. The other chap, whose
whiskered face the lads had recognized
instantly, acted more wisely, hoping, no

doubt, for some moment to arrive where strategy or surprise might count.

"Vat? Eh? Py shoose, you shoot me? Vell, no, you shoot me nod! I vas holt mein hands up so, und shtop poinding dot peestol! Uh! It might vent off!"

"It will sure go off and through your fat gizzard if you don't turn round and head for the road and town! Both of you, now march!"

Don issued this order, then he turned to Mrs. Shultz who had suddenly lifted her voice in a loud lament, much resembling a screech.

"Now, listen, please: Your man must be all right; all we want him for is to tell about this other fellow. Don't worry; he'll be back right soon. Say, Clem, you explain to her; I guess she's going crazy."

This was pretty close to the facts, although long association with the hard knocks of a troubled existence had saved her from going crazy now. But, woman-like, she must fly to the defense of her man, even though, German-like, she was his slave. She was making a vehement protest of some kind, largely by rushing to Shultz and trying to reach her arms around his ample waist; she may have meant to carry him off bodily and protect or hide him, but she fell short in estimating his avoirdupois.

Clem gently pulled the woman back and again reassured her; by insisting about twenty times that it was all right and that she need not worry he managed at last to get her a little calmer and then Don ordered the men forward.

But now the bearded fellow had something to say and it was in the best of English, without a trace of foreign accent. He did not offer to lower his arms.

"I suppose, young gentlemen, this is some kind of a holiday prank; is it not? A schoolboy pleasantry, though rather a severe one, but being once young myself I can sympathize with the exuberance of youth. When you see fit to end this, permit us both and this poor woman to enter the house. I am quite ill and we have all lost much sleep of late. Be then so kind as to—."

"We can imagine that you have indeed lost much sleep and you will probably lose more!" Don was sarcastic. "But we didn't come here to parley. If this is a schoolboy joke it's sure enough a hefty one; all you've got to do is to fall in with it and do as you're told. The next time this gun cracks it's going to be right straight at one of your carcasses, by cracky, and you've going to get hurt! So, hit the road out yonder for town and hit it lively! Get moving, or I'm going to pull this trigger the way she's pointing. Now then, go on!"

"But, my boy, you have no right to thus threaten and order us about. You do not appear like bandits; surely you can mean us no harm and we have done nothing—"

"But we think you have," put in Clem, which was not altogether diplomatic, if it seemed best not to put this man on his guard. Don saw the drift that matters would soon take and parleying was not in order.

"Say, Dutch, listen: You're wrong; we are bandits and this is a real hold-up; see? If you're not the party we want you can hustle back here again, quick."

Shultz put in his inflated oar:

"Bah! You do not vant me. No! I vill not go mit you!"

"Oh, yes you will, or get a lot of lead in you," Don asserted.

"We surely wish you to do just as we say," Clem added. Perhaps it was growing a little hard for him to keep up his courage, but not so with Don; the more that youth was confronted with difficulties, the more determined he became and he was now about as mad as a June hornet.

"Go on out into the road and head for town and no more shenanigan! In two seconds more I'm going to begin shooting and I'd rather kill somebody right now than get a million dollars."

"Now, just a minute, young gentleman." The bearded man's voice was most appealing. "If this is a hold-up and you want money, why then, I can gladly—" The fellow's hand went into his hip pocket and he edged toward Don.

"Back up! Say, by thunder I'm just going to kill you, anyhow!" was Don's reply and upon the instant he almost had to make good his word, for the man leaped right at him, with a snarl resembling that of an angry cat. But the boy was ready and even quicker; dropping the muzzle of his weapon a little he fired and dodged aside at the same time. The man stumbled and fell upon the frozen ground; he floundered a little; then sat up.

"You back up, too, Shultz, or you'll get it! Now, then, Clem, hunt a wheelbarrow and we'll just cart this chap to town, anyway.

You and Shultz can take turns. Hurry,
Clem; there must be one around somewhere.
Go into the house, Mrs, Shultz; we won't
hurt your husband if he doesn't get gay."

CHAPTER V

REWARDED

THE procession that wound out of the
gate, down the road, over the railroad tracks, past the station, into
and along the main street a little way, then
down the broad cross street to the mills was
indeed a queer one; naturally one to draw the
attention of a crowd, if there had been anyone
on the street so early in the morning to see
it. Those who were up and about, who
had not gone back to bed after the explosion,
had stayed at the mill to join in the well-paid-
for work of rehabilitation. or to stand around
and discuss the crime.

When the slow-moving caravan arrived,
after a toilsome trip with many stops for rest,
Clem having been the motive power all the
way for the squeaking, one-wheeled vehicle,
the crowd at the mill paused to observe and
consider this rather startling performance.
Christmas night was one long to be remembered in Lofton.

"Hi! Here comes the circus, the elephant

in the lead!" announced Jimmy West, a
wit among the mill hands, as he caught
sight of the outline of the approaching group.
Shultz marched ahead; then came the wheelbarrow and Clem; then Don, his revolver
ever ready.

"Ah, what—what have you here? What
does this mean, my son?" Mr. Stapley
queried.

"Fer goodness' sake, hit's Dutchy Shultz
an' another feller, thet them there boys hez
brung in!" remarked an ancient citizen.

"Dis vas von outrache, py gollies! I
vill nod—"

"Shut up, Shultz, I told you, or you'll
get plugged yet!" Don threatened. The
crowd did not embarrass him.

"We think this is your dynamiter, Dad,"
Clem stated, calmly. He had had time to
compose himself.

"Eh? What makes you think so?"

"Got a lot of reasons, Dad; a lot of evidence
against this fellow."

"So? But what's the matter with him?"

"Donald shot him. He isn't much hurt,
I guess. But we don't know. We just brought
them along."

"Hey, Mr. Strang, here, evidently, is a

job for you! And we'd better have Doctor
Richards here again."

The town constable clambered out from
among the wreckage of the office building
where he had been searching for clues and
approached. Amid the buzz of remarks and
questions he paused long enough to consider
and then to become somewhat nettled at
what appeared like high-handed proceedings
beyond his authority.

"What's this? You kids make an arrest?
Took a lot on yourselves, I'm thinkin'.
Eh? Shot this fellow? Hello! You Shultz?
Huh! This looks like pretty darned bold
business to me. Put down that gun, young
fellow!" This to Don.

"You go and sit down will you? Maybe
you think I've had no use for this." Don was
still seeing red, but with all of his wits working. "Mr. Stapley, you get busy on this;
you're most interested. This gink," indicating
the constable, "couldn't catch a mudturtle
that had robbed a hen roost in the middle of
the day. There's just one thing to do: bring
the watchman here."

"Put up that gun, I tell you!" ordered
Strang, starting toward Don.

"If you want to fill an early grave you get

gay with me now!" Don said, backing off around the crowd. Mr Stapley interposed.

"Put up your pistol, Donald. We'll take care of this matter now."

"But, Mr. Stapley, Shultz will get away! He and Strang are old cronies. Many a jag Strang got in Shultz's place when he had his saloon; everybody knows that." This caused a general laugh.

"Let him alone, Strang. Perhaps these boys have done us a big service."

"Well, if you think maybe we've got the wrong men, just get the watchman here," Don reiterated.

"Davis went home and to bed," announced a bystander.

"Well, we can wake him; we'll wheel these fellows over there and let him see this one," Don insisted.

Mr. Stapley issued several rapid orders; a big mill hand, grinning, brought up the wheelbarrow and began trundling it and its human freight down the street again. Two others, with a piece of stout twine, noosed Shultz's hands behind him and had him helpless in a moment; then handed him over to Strang, who really would not have dared to be false to his trust. Don, beneath a lamp and before Strang, emptied the cartridges out of his revolver; then handed his weapon to Clem, who also unloaded his gun, and the boys quickly followed on to the watchman's abode.

The ceremony there was as dramatic as could have been wished by the most excitement-loving onlooker. Davis was brought down to the door and he took a look at the two Germans under a bright light. He paused long enough to make his assertion emphatic, pointing his finger and appearing so sure that no one could have doubted him.

"I didn't see Shultz an' I would have knowed him, anyway; he ain't no stranger to nary one in this here town. But I did see that man! He's one o' them that run from the office buildin' acrosst the yard just before the bomb went off. That feller an' another one—a long, thin cuss without any whiskers—they must 'a' set their fuses too short an' was scared, because they skinned out awful quick. Then the thing went off an' the one near where I was a second later, an' it fixed me so's I didn't know nothin'."

"You think that this man—" began Mr. Stapley, indicating the wheelbarrow's passenger who had said no word, but only sat hugging his leg and looking very pale.

"Yes sir, Mr. Stapley, that there feller is one o' the two men I seen. I'm as sure of it as I am that the sun riz yest'day mornin'! I'll take a bunch of oaths on it ez big ez the mill prop'ty! Knowed him soon's I seen him."

"Thank you, Davis. Go back to bed and I hope you're better—"

A cheer, at first uncertain, then growing in volume and intent, interrupted the mill president.

"Hurrah for the kids!" it began; then; "That's the stuff!" "Sure they turned the trick!" "Them kids is some fellers!" and: "Whoop 'em up!" Both boys were caught up on the shoulders of the crowd and passing Strang someone shouted:

"Say, Constable, you ain't got a blamed thing t' say, so shut up!"

"Ben, you and Phil get this fellow down to the mill hospital and stay with him," ordered Mr. Stapley. "The doctor will be here any minute. Mr. Strang, hold on to Shultz; he was giving these men asylum and we all know his sentiments. Better lock him up and we'll work the legal proceedings tomorrow. As for the boys, I won't stand for any action to be taken against them, unless the district attorney insists, and I don't believe he will. They may have exceeded their rights, but you see the result. Good-night, Strang. Come on, men; we'll go back to work. You boys had better go home and get some sleep; you both need it. We'll talk the whole matter over tomorrow."

But when the morrow came, a little late in the morning, the talk was prefaced by a bit of news. A few hours before the bearded German had eluded his jailors just long enough to swallow a dose of poison and he had died in half a minute and almost without a tremor. Prussic acid, Doctor Richards said, and added that the wound inflicted by Don's bullet was a mere flesh scratch in the leg and had only caused a temporary paralysis, largely imaginary. In the darkness the boy had aimed to hit the fellow just above the knee.

They were all at the Stapley mansion, most comfortably seated. The president of the mills and the doctor were old friends. knowing nothing of the long feud between the lads here in the town and at Brighton, and now pleased that the boys had acted together.

"We want to know the whole story;

just how it all happened and all that you did; eh, Doc?" Mr. Stapley demanded.

Between them the boys managed to make a complete narrative, though the latter part of it—the taking of the two Germans and the shooting—Clem told, after much cross-questioning. Mr Stapley then commented:

"It's pretty easy to grasp the merits of this, Doc. My son's part has been anything but that which a proud father could be ashamed of and I'm glad the boy has shown so much nerve and spunk. But it is your son, Donald here, who has really carried the thing through. That boy's going to be a regular young Napoleon one of these days, Doc, you may be sure! Better give his scrapping ability all the development possible."

"Oh, now, Mr. Stapley, I didn't do any more than Clem did. He was right there on the job. Why, he wheeled the wheelbarrow and he—"

"Oh, very good indeed! A rather hard task! But something of a laborer's job wasn't it? You seem to have done—"

"'Comparisons are odious,' Stapley. There's glory enough in this to go round," suggested the doctor.

"Sure, sure, but nevertheless we've got to discriminate when the rewards are forthcoming. Our company is greatly indebted to these boys and so is the country. That fellow might have gotten off and have done a lot more damage, probably to us. Now we've got only one rascal to hunt down. It is wonderful, I must say, very, for boys to have carried this out as you did. Clem, you deserve high praise for getting on to those fellows in the train. But now look here son, the strategy of the actual capture and the nervy manner in which it was carried out seems to have depended mostly upon Donald and I want you to act with me in this matter. The company will reward this act with five hundred dollars and, my boy, in this case I want it all to go to Donald. You shall reap your reward otherwise; I'll see to that in various ways. Of course you're willing?"

"I'm not willing!" spoke up Don and his father shook his head. Clem gazed straight before him with a solemn, hurt expression.

"It must be as I wish," Mr Stapley insisted. "We shall consent to no other arrangement. Doc, I'll send the check to you to bank for your boy, and Donald, I want to thank you for your splendid action in this affair."

CHAPTER VI

DISSENSION

THE end of the holiday week approached and on the day after New Year's there would be again a general migration of eager youths, all over the broad land, into the outstretched arms of alma mater. But competing fiercely with all the institutions of learning, a mightier need beckoned the physically able, for there was work to do to make the "world safe for democracy."

Clement Stapley and Donald Richards heard the call and stopped to consider it. They knew old Brighton was ready to welcome back her knights of brain and brawn, but even more insistently they were aware that far greater institutions controlled by the United States Government were also eager to welcome the same brain and brawn. The Red Cross beckoned them, the Emergency Aid and the Y. M. C. A. wanted the help of strong and willing hands; bigger still loomed the Government itself, with its

demands for men, but with a more urgent
need. Surely Old Brighton could wait and
so could their own desire for learning; at
such a time as this the country, all the world
indeed, blocked some of its wheels of progress
to permit other wheels to turn the faster, to
roll along helpfully, determinedly, to reach
the hilltop of peace at the end of the fierce
journey.

Don sat down to the breakfast table on
Monday morning with four younger boys,
his brothers, all hungry and noisy. The
mother of the Richards boys had long been
dead; the aunt, their father's maiden sister,
who presided over the household, had departed a few minutes before upon some important
errand, leaving the interior to the tender
mercies of the wild bunch who seemed bent
on having an especially merry time, for they
believed the doctor had gone to attend an
urgent case.

Don was the only one of the group who
appeared in no mood to raise a rumpus;
he busily applied himself to satisfying his
very healthy appetite and only switched off
at necessary intervals in the attempt to
enforce peace and to defend himself against
the tussling twins, who would rather scrap

than eat. The other two, one older and one younger, but almost the huskiest of the brothers, insisted on having a hand in these athletic performances. And then there came an unpleasant surprise.

Jim and Jake, the twins, in an effort to compel the surrender of a buttered buckwheat cake, toppled over on Merrill, the second son, who in turn flung them against Ernest. That wily youngster was more than equal to such occasions; he dodged out of his chair and when the struggling twins tumbled across his seat he twisted the corner of the tablecloth about the neck of one, quickly wrecking things, as the wrestlers fell to the floor. Don made a wide grab at several things at once, but finding his attempt futile he turned, tore the tusslers apart and sent them sprawling to opposite corners; then he gave Ernest a crack with open hand, which caused that youngster being the baby of the family, to bawl loudly.

Just at that instant Dr. Richards hurriedly entered the room, for he had just been fixing his auto runabout and now came back for a bite to eat.

The sight that confronted the busy man was enough to exasperate a saint. He saw

Donald in the midst of the mêlée and jumped
at a too hasty conclusion. A man usually
of few words, often over-lenient and generally
just, he now, let his temper run away with
his judgment and his tongue. Grabbing
two dried buckwheat cakes that had, by
merest chance, remained on the edge of the
table, he turned back toward the door.

"You are setting your younger brothers
anything but a good example, Donald! We
have less of this sort of thing when you're
away. If you carry on this way at Brighton
I should think you'd soon be in disgrace.
You ought to be a little older and join the
army; the discipline there would do you
good. A nice breakfast this is!" he added as
he began, moodily, to eat.

Don was too proud and too loyal to the
joint offenders to explain. It seemed enough
for him to know that he was not to blame,
that the scolding was not merited and his
father would soon find this out. An idea had
quickly entered his head.

"I can manage to get into the war, Father,
if you'll sign an application paper."

"Well, I'll see about it—haven't time now."

"Yes, I think you have. Better sign before
we wreck the house, or set fire to it. Here's

the document. Write on the last line, at the bottom."

Doctor Richards seized the paper that Don shoved at him, but hardly glanced at it. "I suppose you feel mightly independent since you got that five hundred dollars. Well, going will probably do you good." With that the man of many duties drew forth his fountain pen, placed the paper against the door-jamb, and quickly wrote his name. "Let me know later just what you intend doing; I will help you all I can. But if you like school best, better go back, perhaps." The doctor stepped out of the room, the front door slammed, there was the chug of a motor and the boys were again left to themselves.

The twins and Ernest sneaked away; Merrill turned to Don, whom he really loved and admired.

"Say, that was rotten! And for me and those kids to let you take that, too! You bet I'll tell Dad all about it when he comes back."

"Well, all right, if you want to; but not now. Not one word before I get off, which will be this afternoon probably. I really can't blame Father much; it was tough for him to miss a decent breakfast and he has a lot to put up with from us kids—with all he does for us! But he won't be bothered with me for a while and if I get over there maybe he will never again be bothered with me. Well, I'll see you later, Mel, and let you know. I'm off to see Clem Stapley now; perhaps he will be going, to."

But on his way Don stopped at the Army and Red Cross recruiting station, in the same busy office, being received with much gusto, both because of his recent heroic conduct in landing the German agent and of his frank engaging manner. He had much to say, found much to learn and got what he was after. Then he climbed the hill toward the Stapley mansion. Clem was at the garage, helping the chauffeur tinker with a crippled motor.

"Hello, old man!" shouted Don, but he noticed that the older lad hardly turned his head. He seemed much interested in his task. "Well, what's the good word?" continued the visitor. "Anything new?"

"Don't know a thing," answered Clem, without looking up.

"Well, things are coming my way," Don said.

"Yes, I notice," Clem agreed, with a sneer on his face, "and you're not dodging them very hard, either."

"I was speaking of Government duties," Don offered, ill at ease. He had been satisfied that the old ill feeling had been completely patched up, between Clem and himself, by the heroic episode through which they had just passed, for his own feeling was friendly. But surely Clem's manner was cool, even more curt than before. However, in the last remark the older lad showed some interest.

"How do you mean, 'Government duties'?" he asked.

"I've just joined the Red Cross ambulance service, Clem. Leave tonight. Thought you'd like to know—"

"I enlisted with the Marines two days ago," Clem announced rather coolly.

"Good for you! Hurrah! When do you go? We might—"

But Clem, who had turned back to work on the car said curtly:

"When I get ready. In a few days, perhaps."

"No chance, then, for us to get away together?"

"None in the least."

"Well, I'm glad you got in. Of course you had no trouble. Your father gave his—"

"Look here, Richards!" Clem turned toward the younger boy almost savagely. "I don't see that you need to concern yourself with what I've done, or doing. As for Dad, you ought to he satisfied after what you got out of the company."

"Oh! So that's what's the matter with you, eh? Sore about that; are you? Well, you know I wanted to divide; I wanted to be fair to you. It was not my—"

"I didn't see you breaking any bones in an effort to be fair."

"If you say I didn't want to be fair, that I was entirely satisfied in taking all that money, then, Stapley, you lie!"

"Say, before I'll take much of that from you I'll punch your head!"

"So? Well, the nose is right here when you want to punch it. Come and punch it! But you won't punch anything. You think you're some fighter. Come on and punch once; just once!"

Clem was no coward and he possessed the cool judgment of a capable boxer. Moreover, he was taller, with a longer reach than Don. But he had to reckon with superior weight, probably greater strength and what counts more than all else—an indomitable spirit. Long brooding over what he considered an injustice on Don's part in accepting all the reward for arresting the Germans, and for permitting others to give him more of the credit for personal bravery had made young Stapley more of an enemy than he had ever been.

How the fight would have ended was not to be known, however, for though Clem would have struck Don, he was prevented by the chauffeur who was by no means to be lightly reckoned with.

"Gwan, now, Clement, me boy! An' you, too, young feller! I'll mop up the floor here with both o' you if you begin scratchin' an' bitin'! What would Mr. Stapley, me boss, say to me if I let you chaw each other up? Gwan, young feller!"—this to Don. "An' you come here, Clement, an' I'll show you the true insides o' this critter, from piston head to crank shaft."

Don took this for both good advice and a logically sound invitation and turned on his heel. But he could not help feeling sorry that again Clem Stapley and himself were "at outs".

CHAPTER VII

GETTING IN

CAMPS and training schools, learning how and drilling. This was the lot of Young America in the latter days of the year 1917 and in the earlier months of the succeeding year, a year long to be remembered and to cut a mighty figure in the history of the United States.

Bloody are the annals of this year of 1918, severe the sacrifices that led the nation into its tragic paths of glory, but so noble and just has been the purpose behind our act of war and so humane our conduct that the whole sane world has applauded. All honor to the fighters first and all praise to the men and the women, young and old, who aided and encouraged the fighters with abundant humanity at home and on the field of strife.

We think of war and see its tragedies mostly through the eyes of the military, but to some of the unarmed participants have come the bitterest experiences and the opportunities for the bravest deeds.

Donald Richards, late student at old Brighton and now Red Cross ambulance driver, too young to enlist as a soldier, but nevertheless keen for action and to do his bit and his best, at once so interested his superiors that after he had fully qualified they quickly placed him where his craving for thrills and work worth while should be amply satisified. In February, after a month of training he sailed across the big pond in a transport laden with troops and met no mishaps on the way.

Three weeks after landing in France the boy found himself in the midst of military activities and the most urgent hospital work. He was clad to his own satisfaction, mostly at his own expense, in khaki. He had become a capable mechanic on automobiles, was well practised in roughing it, in picking his way in strange country, and above all in the fine art of running, with wounded passengers, swiftly and smoothly over rough roads.

First as an assistant driver, then with a car of his own and a helper, he had been assigned to duty along the great highway leading from Paris to Amiens. Like many others in the area of military activity, this road had been well built, rock-ballasted

and hammered hard with normal travel,
in the days before the world war, but now,
from the wheels of great munition trucks
and motor lorries, the wear and tear of marching feet and from little care after long rains,
it had been soaked into a sticky mass, with
a continuation of holes and ruts, puddles
and upheavals. A cross-road led from the
Amiens highway straight east toward the
battle front and into the wide territory
of France held by the enemy. The German
front line was not more than seven miles
from the evacuation hospitals on this cross-
road. These centers of mercy were where
the badly wounded were sent for quick,
emergency operations, which saved many
lives. Between these evacuation hospitals
and the Red Cross base hospital in an old
chateau a few miles outside of Paris and also
near the Amiens road the comparatively
few Red Cross cars and the score or more
of Army ambulances plied almost contin-
uously when there was anything doing at
the front. And for the most part there was
something doing.

From the twenty-first of March, when the
terrific drive of the Huns carried them nearly
to Amiens, and during which time they

occupied Montdidier, until the middle of June, there was pretty constant shelling and scrapping throughout this area. The great German offensive began in March, only a few days before Donald Richards started to run his own ambulance, so that almost his first duties were most urgent and strenuous.

"Whatever the Doctor, Major Little, in command up there, tells you to do, do it," was the order the boy received from the chief at the base hospital, "but your regular duty is to bring the wounded from the evacuation hospitals, or from the dressing stations to us, when so ordered. Of course, we don't want to subject our men to the danger of going up to the lines any more than is absolutely necessary, and we surely do not want you to get hurt, my boy, but this war and the call of duty must be heeded first. Either the surgeons at the dressing stations or Major Little and his assistants at the cross-roads hospitals will tell you where to take the wounded. Critical cases are first operated on at the evacuation hospitals so as to save time, but shell shock, slight wounds, men not very seriously gassed, and merely sick men are brought here direct

from the field. Hence it will be best for you,
if there are no wounded to be brought away
from the evacuation hospitals, to go to the
dressing stations or into a battle area, to
get the wounded in your car anyway you
can. For the most part they will be brought
to you by stretcher bearers; of course, some
will come themselves. I see you have on
your steel helmet. Wear it regularly.

"You must prepare yourself for some
horrible sights, my boy. Above all things,
no matter how much you may be scared,
and you will be, don't lose your nerve. No
one, especially at your age, can be blamed
for being somewhat flabbergasted under fire,
while seeing men killed, maimed, blown to
bits by shells, and all that sort of thing,
but you must try to overcome this. And
be sure to have your gas-mask always handy.

"Now then, have everything in tiptop
shape according to our methods; you had
better take a hot bath, wear clean under-
clothing and brush your teeth. Get a good
meal and be sure to take a lot of chocolate
with you to give out where needed, You
should also have extra blankets in case
you get hurt, or your car crippled and you
have to sleep out. The weather is moder-

ating now and I think it will continue so,
but there will be cold rains. Now then,
be off in an hour and good luck to you!"

From such a general order, Don saw clearly
enough that he would be his own boss a
great deal of the time, and that much of his
most important work must be carried on
according to his own judgment. The boy of
sixteen, who had never really engaged in
anything more strenuous than mere sport,
except the arresting of the German spy
back home, was now brought face to face
with the duties and responsibilities that
were fully man-size.

Don prepared himself quickly for any
undertaking that might be before him. He
made everything ready as the chief had
suggested. He insisted also that the same
be done by his helper, Billy Mearns, a city-
bred young man who was just now getting
familiar with handling and repairing a motor
car.

Presently they started. The little truck, new,
smooth-running and responsive, delighted the
boy. His first duties as helper had been in a
rattletrap machine, which ran only when it
felt like it and in which they carried convalescents from the base hospitals to a place with

terraced gardens and verandas two hundred miles farther south.

Don's new duties exhilarated him and as he turned his car northward he could have said, with Macduff, when that warrior sought to meet Macbeth, the master war-maker: "That way the noise is. Tyrant show thy face!" for, boy-like, yet with a thorough understanding of the situation, secretly desirous of taking some part—he did not know what—in the fighting, he had smuggled a sporting rifle into his car, and he carried a long-barreled revolver in a holster on his hip.

"You see," he confided to Billy Mearns— they called each other by their first names almost from the moment of meeting—"we don't know what we are up against, and I hope I may be hanged, drawn and quartered, as the old pirates used to say, if I let any blamed Hun sneak around me without trying to see if he is bullet-proof."

"Right-o!" agreed Mearns. "But, for goodness' sake, don't get too anxious and take some of our Yanks for Heinies! If you do and I'm along, me for wading the Atlantic right back home! They'd do worse than hang, draw and quarter us; mebbe they'd even pull out our hair or tweak our noses."

"Pshaw! Anybody who couldn't tell a Hun, day or night, ought to have—"

"His nose examined, eh? Oh, you sauerkraut and onions!"

CHAPTER VIII

In it

PLOOF! Ploof! Bang! P-ssst, wam! Zing, zing, zing! T-r-r-r-r-r—rip! Ploooof! Something of this nature, if it can at all be conveyed by words, came in waves, roars and spasms of sound to the ears of Don and Billy, as their ambulance truck traversed part of the five or six miles of cross-road between the evacuation hospitals near the Amiens road, not twenty miles south of that shell-torn town, and the front line of the Allied army where American troops, newly arrived from training camps, were brigaded with the French soldiers; that is, a number of regiments of one nation were included with those of the other in the same sector, sometimes companies, even platoons, of Americans and French fighting side by side against the savage attacks of an enemy far superior in numbers.

"We've just sent a dozen or more to your people down there—nearly all light cases—but there's been some sort of a scrap over

toward the southeast. You can't find a
road, for the enemy holds that, but you can
turn in across the fields to your right, or
follow an old farm road; one of our men
did so yesterday. It is just beyond, where
some reserves are digging in by the edge
of a ruined farm; both the house and barn
have been struck by shells or sky bombs. If
you can go any farther from there you'll
have to ask your way, but probably the
P. C. beyond won't let you go on. There
are two dressing stations to the west of some
woods on a low hill; that will be still farther
to your right as you follow the new trail.
Go to it!"

This was the all-too-brief order Don
received from Major Little, the hospital-
chief when the lads reached the broad tents
on the cross-road early one morning. Without further words Don leaped into his car
and glided on along the narrow road for
about two miles; then he began dodging
shell holes, one here that involved half of
the wheel tracks, another, farther on, which
took in all of the road and had been partly
filled and partly bridged with timbers from
an old building near. Beyond this, small
shell-holes had torn up the once smooth

surface here and there. After the ambulance had traversed another mile, at the best speed possible over such a highway, it overtook a string of ammunition trucks going into position, ready for progress or retreat. Dodging around these and avoiding other shell-holes was difficult for the half mile on to where the artillery had debouched. Once, not two hundred feet ahead, a big shell came over with a swish and snarl and landed in the field near the road, sending up a cloud of sod, dirt and stones and sprinkling the ambulance and its drivers with bits of gravel. One sizable stone landed on the hood with a whang and bounced against the windshield just hard enough to crack it, exactly in line with Billy Mearns' face.

"Pal, we seem to be under fire," remarked Don, and Billy, with a grunt of relief, replied:

"Yes, and if that glass hadn't been there I'd have bitten that stone in half to show I didn't care whether it came this way or not. But say, if we'd been just where that shell landed we would have had to sing Tosti's 'Good-bye.' They're rude things, aren't they, the way they mess up the landscape?"

Don glanced at his smiling companion.

A fellow who could take such matters so calmly, and jest over them, was a lad after his own heart.

The sound of fighting came to the boys now with increasing fury. They were not experienced enough to tell whether it was a regular battle, or merely a skirmish. Anyway, it was lively enough for an introduction to green hands far from home.

They came to where the reserve regiment was digging in. Some of them camped in the open, with a few little canopy tents spread. A few fires were burning. A few officers stood or squatted around talking and laughing. Sentries were pacing up and down. A sentinel stood in the road and faced about toward them, but when he saw the Red Cross on the front and side of the car and had scanned the faces of the drivers he asked no questions but let them pass. Don slowed up enough to hear him say:

"All right. Go find 'em, bo! There's some down there."

"Going to give your friends, the Limburgers, a warm reception after while?" Billy called back and the soldier nodded briskly, smiling and waving his hand.

Turning sharply and dashing along the

old farm road between greening fields, the little car gained a slight crest and, uncertain for the moment which way to turn, Don stopped her. Billy leaned out and looked around.

"Over there are the woods the Major spoke about," he said.

"Sure is. We can cross this meadow, I guess."

"Ooh! Hold on a bit, and look up, Don!"

Two airplanes were circling overhead. The boys could see a black Maltese cross on the under side and near the end of each wing of one plane; the other bore a broad tri-colored circle in similar positions. The two soaring, roaring, vulture-like things were approaching each other, suddenly little jets of white smoke burst from each and long streaks of pale light, like miniature lightning. shot from each flying-machine to the other.

"A Hun plane and a Britisher! It's a fight!" Don remarked excitedly. "See, they're the illuminated bullets to tell just where they're shooting, like squirting a hose. Watch 'em, Billy; watch 'em! Oh, by cracky!"

"Watch them? Do you think I'm taking a nap? Oooh! Look at that gasoline swallow dive! And bring up, too!" The German

plane had done this to try to get around
under the tail of its opponent before the
other could turn, but its calculation went
amiss. The Englishman instantly made a
quick swerve around and then dived straight
at his enemy, sending a stream of bullets
ahead, and as the boche had by this time
turned around and was coming back toward
him, it looked terribly like there would be a
collision.

But not so. The superior maneuvering
of the Britisher was too much for his
antagonist—the Hun plane swerved to the
left, went on straight for a moment, then
began to tilt a little sidewise and to spin
slowly. As it sank it pitched from side to
side, following a spiral course, thus imitating
perfectly the fall of a dead leaf; so perfectly,
indeed, that as it neared the earth and was
not checked not righted it became evident
that the engine had stopped and that the
airman could not control the plane. Then,
when not more than fifty feet above the
ground it suddenly tilted over forward and
crashed to the ground in the field, about
an eighth of a mile beyond the boys.

Looking aloft, then, Don and Billy saw
the victorious English plane going straight

away at high speed toward the enemy's
lines and rising higher in air at every second.

"Work cut out for us right ahead there,"
Don remarked, as he settled back in his
seat and began to speed up his motor. "We
didn't think that our first '*blessé*' would be
a Hun, did we?"

"No. What's a '*blessé*'?"

"Why, I think that's what the French
call a wounded man. I hear them using
it that way."

"I know a little French, but very little;
I hadn't heard that expression before. Many
of these war-time French words bother me
muchly. Look out; another shell-hole! Say,
this must be a regular farm."

They saw the house standing in a clump
of trees. The roadway led straight past it;
with increased speed the ambulance flew by
and in a little while came to the fallen
airplane.

The winged intruder, 'winged' also as a
flying game bird is by the accurate fire of a
sportsman, lay twisted, beyond repair, its
wings, uprights and stays crushed and broken.
Almost beneath the flattened wheels on the
other side, crumpled up on the ground, lay
the unconscious airman. He had either leaped

at the last moment, landing almost where the airplane had, or he had been jarred from his seat by the impact.

The boys were out of the car and beside him at once. Observing that he still breathed, they gently turned him over, trying to find where he was injured; then they saw a mass of clotted blood on his shoulder and discovered the bullet hole.

First Aid was in order. Don ran to the ambulance and returned with a kit. Billy followed to unfasten a stretcher and a blanket. With utmost care, yet moving swiftly, though both lads were admittedly nervous over their first case, they got him on the stretcher, removed his upper garments, bathed the wound, plugged it with antiseptic gauze and then, covering him with the blanket, slid the stretcher into the car.

What next to do? There was room for two or three more; why return with but one? And just beyond here lay the dressing stations, which they could reach in less than two minutes. Don made up his mind quickly and drove the car farther down the narrow farm road and over another field—a pasture. Half way across and toward them, four men were walking in single file. The boys

had just made out that these were stretcher-
bearers when suddenly the men stopped,
ducked down and the foremost one raised
his arm signaling for the car to stop. The
next instant they were hidden from view
by a fountain of earth between them and the
ambulance and not over seventy-five feet
from the car. The earth shook with the
tremendous concussion of the explosion. It
was one of the largest shells. The ambulance
was stopped as though it had butted into
a stone wall; Don felt a mass of glass fly
against him and the car lifted partly up and
swung aside. When he regained his senses
and could see about him through the settling
cloud of dust, he discovered that the car
had been flung crosswise, that the windshield was smashed, and that the top was
bent back, and very much askew. Billy,
not having a grip on a steering wheel, as
Don had, and having partly risen, was now
on his back on the bottom of the car, behind
the seat, his long legs sticking out over the
back. He regained his normal position only
by turning a back somersault and climbing
forward. That the lads were not hurt was
almost a miracle.

But strangest of all was the fact that the

THE AMBULANCE WAS STOPPED AS THOUGH IT HAD BUTTED
INTO A STONE WALL.

tail doors had been blown open, the stretcher lifted out on the ground as neatly as though human hands had done it and looking back Don saw the German airman, shocked into consciousness, sitting up and gazing at him.

CHAPTER IX

Reprisals

BILLY, you aren't kilt entirely, eh? Well, then, hop out and crank her; maybe that volcano didn't stall her. We'll turn round, if she runs, and hunt for those stretcher chaps; guess we can find 'em. Say, I'll bet they're sorry they saw us coming."

"No, for here they come again! It could not have reached them. Oooh, but wasn't it a daisy? For about one second I longed to be back in the good, old United States. Hah! Wait till I spin her. There she goes as fine as a handorgan!"

Don backed and turned the car; then the lads went to the German.

"Well, Fritz, feel better?" Don asked, speaking English.

No answer; a blank stare. Billy comprehended and at once got some fun out of the incident. It was a funereal affair that didn't have a humorous side for him. He held his spread hand, palm down, over his

head, moved it about like the flying of an
airplane, pointed to it and to the Hun with
his other finger; then making the hand
take a big drop through the air and double
up on the ground again pointed to the airman.
The latter understood at once and scowled
at his combined rescuers and captors; then
flopped back on the stretcher. The boys
restored him to his place in the car and turned
to meet the men from the dressing-station.
They all looked fagged out, tired beyond
endurance. As a matter of fact, they were to
keep on many more hours longer. Their
conversation was brief, but to the point.

"Red Cross? Get these men back as quickly
as you can and return at once. We are in
an *abri* there by the woods. Tell Major
Little that the lieutenant wants more ambulances right away. We have eleven wounded;
two 'going West.'"

"All right. I'll put the juice to her, Sergeant?" Don saw the three bent stripes on
the man's sleeve. The four shifted the
wounded, one of whom was unconscious,
to the unfolded white stretchers of the car,
strapped them down, folded their own brown
army stretchers and turned back.

"What does he mean by 'going West'?"

Billy whispered, as they got under way.

"Dying," replied Don. "Guess it's an Indian phrase—'toward the setting sun.' Poor chaps!"

"O my! I'm afraid one of these," Billy pointed his thumb over his shoulder, "won't stay 'East' long. I hope he does, but you see, I really ought to study medicine. I get hunches about that sort of thing, you know."

They flew over the even ground, and moved slowly over the rough. Again in the farm road they were swiftly passing the house when a cry from one of their passengers arrested their attention. It was a cry for water.

Don pressed down his brake and turned to Billy. "That canteen—" he began.

"I think that a real cold drink," suggested the young man, "would do more good. Oughtn't they to have a well here? Suppose I see."

"We'll both go and get a pull, too; then bring some back. Come on!" Don said.

The quaint little half-stone domicile, in the very midst of this shell-torn area, faced directly east; the rear was, therefore, away and thus somewhat sheltered from the enemy's

lines. There had been a French or American
dressing station in the front room, but a
German 77-m. shell had come along and
demolished the wall and a portion of the
interior. The boys quickly passed under
the newly leafing fruit trees, where bird
arrivals were singing, and reached the rear
of the house. Here, in the mellowing spring-
time warmth, an old woman and an old man
were sitting; the one on the door step,
the other, upon an ancient stone seat, leaning his head on his cane. By the side of the
old woman's knee a little child of about
four years gazed up at the visitors with
wide-open, blue eyes.

Don, knowing no French and forgetting
that Billy knew a little, resorted to panto-
mime. He made a cup of his hand and lifted
it to his lips; the old man pronounced the
word water very distinctly and pointed to
a well-sweep among the shrubbery. While
Don drew forth a moss-covered bucket of
water that looked sparkling, Billy was recall-
ing his school-day language and getting
information. Yes, the old couple were trust-
ing in the mercy of a Higher Power; if
it were His will to take them, well and good,
but they hoped it would be quick and without

suffering. Rather than leave their lifetime
abode, where they had always known comfort and happiness, they would risk the
present dangers, which they hardly seemed
to realize. They would dare almost anything rather than wander to strange regions.

And here was little Marie, happy with
her grandparents, though her father had
died in the war and her mother from grief
and illness soon after. Well, the good General
Foch, now that he had been made commander
of all the armies, would soon chase the wicked
boches away. The French would fight on
forever, and so would the good English.
And then the Americans were coming, they
said. Were the young men English?

American! "*Vive l' Amerique!*" Ah, it
was good to see them. And how soon, oh,
how soon would the great army arrive and
rid France, dear, suffering, half-destroyed
France, from the wicked, hateful boches?
"*A bas les boches!*"

Don had taken water to the wounded
men, two of whom received it eagerly;
the other lay in a stupor. The passengers,
the boy now saw, were two Frenchman,
besides the German airman.

"Come on, Billy!" Don called, and shaking

hands with the old people and lifting the child for a kiss, hastened away. As he leaped into the machine and Billy ran to the front end, grasping the crank, they heard again, now not high overhead, the roar of a flying motor and there came an airplane, marked with the black Maltese cross, sailing across their road and very nearly over them.

"I guess he can see our Red Cross sign," Billy said, but Don, having heard many stories, was taking no chances; he started and flew swiftly down the road. Blam! Something exploded far behind them and to one side of the road. Again, within a few seconds, another detonation, much nearer, came to their ears. Billy was craning his neck out of the side of the car.

"He's after us! Would you think it? I suspect he'll get us, too, unless we beat him out to the soldiers. They've got anti-aircraft guns, haven't they, Don?"

"Sure, and he's got to go some. Just watch us!"

It was a race for a few seconds, though the airman must have been wary, flying low as he did. He could not gain on the car, and soon, with a long sweep, he was turning back, flying now even lower. Where were

6

the Allied airmen? Not one in sight! As
Don neared the main road again and reached
the little hillock he slowed up, on hearing
the crack of light artillery in the fields.
The anti-aircraft guns had got busy and the
Hun had reason to keep his distance. But
if he was foiled in his attempt to wreck an
Allied Red Cross ambulance he surely meant
to find some prey for his perverted desire to
destroy. He had seen the place from where
the ambulance had started as he approached;
certainly there must be a dressing station
in the little farm house.

Billy, looking back then, saw it. The
muderous Hun flew lower still over the
spot of peacefulness and beauty; if he had
any sense of pastoral loveliness, hate and the
German desire for mastery had drowned it
all. Something falling straight down from the
airplane passed exactly over the little stone
and frame dwelling and then a great column
of flame, of black and gray smoke, of stones
and bits of splintered wood leaped upward
and sunk to earth again. A cloud of smoke
and dust drifted away in the wind.

"Oh, Don! The house, the old people,
the little girl!" said Billy with a sob, and
Don, clamping down his brakes, gazed at

his companion. It was the first time he had seen him with anything different from a smile on his gentle face, even when danger was literally heaped up in front of them. But now the young man's soft eyes had a horror in them and a gray pallor had taken the place of the pink, almost girlish complexion.

Don looked back and saw the holocaust wrought by the Hun.

"That—that murderous devil!" he exclaimed.

The wounded airman in the car turned his face toward Don and made a remark in German, probably not expecting it to be understood. Don replied in German:

"One of your airmen has blown up the little farmhouse where we got the drink! No doubt the good people are killed!"

"But it is war and a good hit is to be praised. Besides, these degenerate French—"

Don turned on the fellow with the glare of an angry wildcat; in his excitement his German mostly gave way to English:

"What's that? *You teufel! You* say that! And when we are treating you decently? Well, we shall just fix you, you—!"

"Oooh, Don! Look, look!"

The airman had once more turned about, evidently to fly back over his work of destruction to feast his eyes on its completeness. Then he met his Waterloo. The long swerves took him beyond and near the woods, where a French 75, aimed by a cool-headed American gunner barked upward just once. With a burst of flame the airplane pitched to the earth. The brutal driver, who refused to respect an ambulance, a supposed dressing station, or the modest home of non-combatants, was probably strapped on his seat and unable to extricate himself went down to the most horrible of deaths.

"Ah, he got his, all righty!" Don shouted; then turning: "And here's another who's going to get his! Billy, this Hun, this skunk here, is praising the act of that devil! We'll just dump him out and let him lie here and suffer and bleed to death. Come on; give a hand!"

"No, no, Don! You can't mean that. It would not be humane."

"Humane? I'd be humane to a dog, a cat, a worm even, I hope, but not to a thing like this. Come—!"

"'As they should do unto you', Don. I know this is war and he's a Hun, but it's all the more of an excuse that he is only partly human; he doesn't know any better and he has feelings, some. Let's go on, Don, please, now." Don leaped to his seat with Billy and they continued on their way.

CHAPTER X

ZEALOUS BILLY

MAJOR LITTLE ordered the German airman turned over to an army ambulance where he would be disposed of as a wounded man and prisoner. To Don the surgeon said, after hearing the boy's message:

"Yes, we have had the same over the wire, but could hardly get it. Hurry back, then. I'll send two others after you. Phoned for them an hour ago. Look out for gas shells; they may be sending them over soon. Listen for the warning gongs from our trenches and the gurgling sound of the shells themselves—you'll know it. Or you may see the fumes drifting your way in certain lights; after the explosion, sometimes, you can see them very plainly. You can generally smell the fumes in the open before they come near enough to injure you—then on with your masks! By the way," the Major lowered his voice, "is that helper of yours on the job?"

"Yes, sir; you may be sure he is! As cool and not afraid as they make 'em." Don was glad of this chance to praise Billy. His regard for the youth was hardly less than a strong love for his pal. The doctor seemed surprised.

"I would hardly have thought that," he admitted, —"a gentle kind of a boy. But that kind often fools you. Even girls themselves—some of our demurest nurses are the bravest under fire. Well, I'm glad you like him. Now, you must make a quick get-away!"

Don and Billy boarded their little car again, and just as they were turning around, two other ambulances dashed up. The first one was a light army truck, manned by members of the regular corps of the army service. The other bore the Red Cross and it looked like a higher grade of car than that commonly in use by that organization. Don was swinging into the road and just caught sight of the driver and helper in this last car. But as he glanced at the side face of the former a rush of partial recognition mixed with an undefined feeling of hostility swept over him. Where had he seen that face before? There were not many persons he remembered unpleasantly. He had been in one or two student rows with ruffians, who had fared badly as a rule and the boys at Old Brighton had it in for a disagreeable fellow who was even opposed to their speaking above a whisper when they passed his place in the town. The face he had just seen was not one of these. Well, there was more big work cut out ahead and he would think over this question later. Yet the matter kept returning to his mind in spite of the battle sounds and sights, among which they soon came at close quarters.

"I can't understand one thing:" Billy remarked, as they sped on. "Why is the shooting so at random? Just look at the shells that have landed all around us, in the fields, in the roads, almost everywhere, doing no real damage, except to stir up the ground, hitting hardly anyone. It looks like fool business to me."

"And when you think how much one of these shells costs and how much must be paid for a hundred rounds of cartridges fired by a machine-gun, no wonder they say that it costs a good many thousands of dollars for every man that gets hit," Don offered.

"Well, if it costs so much I wish they'd

save those that come my way. I'd just as
lief treat even the Huns more economically!"
declared Billy.

Don had to laugh, though at the moment
they were approaching again the old farm
house, now torn to pieces, where the Hun
airman had dropped his bomb but an hour
before. Billy also noticed it and asked Don
to stop.

"Couldn't we go in and see, Don? It will
be solemn enough, but we can be sure they're
all—they're not suffering."

The boys alighted and rounded the house
once more, stepping over broken bits of stone
and mortar and twisted framing. Billy was
ahead and he took but one glance and turned
about.

"Beyond doubt. They had at least their
wish not to suffer." He uttered the words
like a funeral benediction, and followed Don
back. As they were about to emerge from
the trellised gateway the other Red Cross
ambulance shot by, the occupants, no doubt,
supposing those in the boys' car had stopped
here for a drink. Again Don caught sight
of the driver of that car. Instantly it came
to the boy who the fellow must be. The
recognition was quite complete—and startling.

Don stood in the road, looking after the speeding car. Billy's thoughts were upon other matters. The ambulance ran on until almost out of sight. Then suddenly, instead of turning across toward the dressing station at the western edge of the woods, it veered to the east across fields and ran down a slope to a clump of bushes and low trees where it stopped. The boy wondered if there could be a dressing station at that spot.

"Don, if you can go on just this once without me, I'd like to stay and bury that poor old couple and the little girl. It seems horrible to let them lie there, exposed, uncared for, as though they had no friends. What do you say?"

"All right, Billy you stay. I can make the trip alone. They'll help me with the *blessés* at the station and at the hospital too. If anything does happen to me—should I get hit—you couldn't help much until you got the hang of running over such roads. And say, Billy, you can do something else: when you hear a car going back take a peep and if it's those fellows that just went by, observe them; will you? If you see them coming, go out and stop them and ask who they are; you can let on you're making a report.

I'm just curious. Tell you why later. G'bye! I'll stop for you on the next trip down."

Don dashed on, reached the dressing station without mishap, took on two wounded *poilus* and one Yank; they sped back.

Billy quickly found a garden spade and went to work with all his might so as to complete his gruesome task. The ground was soft beneath a wide-spreading apple tree just showing signs of blossoming; a sweet-voiced bird sang the while in the branches above, and this was the only requiem the old couple and the little child should know, as, wrapped carefully in sheets rescued from the destroyed house, they filled the one grave.

The tender-hearted youth's eyes were wet while he labored for the poor souls who deserved a better burial than this. When the grave was filled he made a rude cross of boards and wrote on it a simple inscription, a tribute from his own gentle heart.

This was the best the boy could do. The little bird still sang its cheery ditty overhead. He turned away with a sigh and said, half aloud:

"I wonder what Father would think of me now. He wouldn't believe it possible of his youngest boy he used to call 'a silly, girl-like thing.' I couldn't blame him then, but now—well, he'll change his mind about me if I go back—that is, *if* I get back."

Then Billy heard a car approaching and slipped out front to take a look, as Don had requested. It was the army ambulance returning. But where was the other Red Cross ambulance?

Well, Don would not be here again for perhaps half an hour yet. There would be time to slip along the road and get a glimpse of the other car. Then he might give his pal even more information than he expected.

The clump of bushes was not more than three hundred yards from the farm road and if there was a dressing station there Billy would find it out—the information might be of value. To keep out of sight of Hun airmen, should they fly overhead, the youth followed close to the line of low evergreen trees that skirted the road and when he reached the end of these but stood still within their welcome shadow, he gazed across at the clump. In all this section of land north of the distant woods and between where the American regiment in reserve on the cross-road was stationed, there were no troops.

Evidently it was not a spot where the Huns could break through because of the strongly entrenched positions of the Allies facing them. There had been some Hun raids and some Allied counter-attacks, platoons of Americans fighting beside the French—hence the wounded. But the Germans had not succeeded in pushing their line any farther than the western outskirts of the small village of Cantigney, another half mile east of this ground. Here had come to an end the German drive around Montdidier, a part of the Amiens offensive during the early spring, which is called the first great drive of 1918. The effort to take Amiens, a few miles to the north, was to meet defeat about two weeks later. And meanwhile the great armies intrenched themselves, crouching like lions at bay. They almost ceaselessly growled with their numerous artillery and every little while kept up the clawing and biting through local raids and counter-attacks, adding constantly to the wounded and the dead.

It was strange, Billy thought, if there should be a dressing station here. He had been told that the stream, the south fork of the Avre, bent here to the west and that the German positions followed the river at this

point. Therefore, while the Allied reinforce-
ment was stronger against attack, the Huns
had made themselves stronger also, to match
their opponents and the local fights were
all the fiercer, therefore making the wide
expanse of low land sloping toward the stream
subject to continual bombardment from higher
and overplaced shot and shell. It was across
this area that the ambulances were forced
to travel from the dressing stations in the
shelter of the hillside woods beyond. That
was dangerous enough without the further
exposure of a dressing station, even in a
well covered *abri*, or dugout, to this zone
of flying shells.

But what could the men with this ambulance be about for such a length of time,
when they were probably sent to the other
dressing station to bring away the wounded?
Surely they had met with some urgent
call here. Billy pondered. Might he not go
over and aid them?

He started on a swift trot and had covered
more than half the distance in less than half
a minute when a thing occurred that made
him drop to a walk, watching, wondering.
Out of a thicket a tiny puff of white smoke
rose in jets, as though measured by time;

two close together, then four, then two, then six, then one, then six again and 2-6-6-3-2-6-4-4-2-6-3 and so on for another half minute. By that time Billy had stopped. Was it mere instinct that made him dodge back of a wide bush and peer through its budding branches?

Again the funny little jets of white smoke. Why were they doing this—these Red Cross men? There was the ambulance itself, in plain sight, by the edge of the thicket and, moreover, a Red Cross sign had been raised on a pole above the low trees.

Billy's eyes rapidly scanned the surroundings. A line of trees on the slope toward the south shut off the thicket from the view of the woods and the low ground here could not well be seen by the reserves back on the cross-road. It seemed a place that might be well chosen for isolation, if desired. And high in air, far over the enemy's trenches, a Hun observation balloon could be plainly seen against the white, cumulous clouds.

Billy gazed at this object long and keenly. He could distinctly discern the basket beneath it; he could detect a certain movement of something white going up and down, up and down several times and then a pause;

then several times again. While this was
going on the puffs of white smoke from
the thicket were not forthcoming. Then,
when the while thing at the balloon ceased
to move, the puffs began again.

What did all this mean? Could there be
any connection between the thicket and the
balloon—the little puffs of white smoke
and the movements of that white thing by
the basket in the sky?

Well, he was going to find out, anyway.
There seemed to be nothing else he could
do that would straighten out the mystery
in his own mind. And so he again trotted
forward direct toward the thicket, still watching the balloon. Suddenly he grasped the
truth. There were two upward sweeps of
white in the sky and instantly the little
puffs ceased again. The two men, wheeling
about, their heads above the bushes, saw
Billy and began to beckon him. Fearless,
probably without any misgivings regarding
himself, he went on to join them. One pointed
to the balloon and said something about it
and Billy gazed at it again, entirely off his
guard. Suddenly he ceased to see anything;
he only tossed his arms feebly in air and sunk
to the ground in a crumpled heap. In front

of him the long, thin-faced, narrow-eyed driver of the car seized again a queer looking instrument and began quickly to shoot up more of the little smoke puffs. Back of the fallen youth stood the helper, holding a heavy iron rod in his hand. He made a quick, excited remark to the driver in German.

CHAPTER XI

"GONE WEST"

ONCE again along the farm road came Don's ambulance. It reached the old farm house and stopped. He called loudly for Billy Mearns. There was no answer and Don rose in his seat to go and look for his pal, and to witness the good work he had done here. Always alert, he glanced about. He had not met the other Red Cross ambulance again. Was it still in the low ground by the thicket?

It was, and the men there were moving about. Don stood watching them for a moment. He saw a slender figure, one that he surely recognized as that of Billy Mearns, crossing the field toward the thicket. He saw two men within the clump and when Billy reached the bushes and passed among them Don saw one of the men lift his arm as if he were pointing.

Then, for an instant, Don's heart seemed to stand still, for he saw the other man who had been in the clump of bushes raise his arm, holding some sort of weapon and strike the slender figure down.

The army ambulance at this moment was also coming along the farm house lane. The driver and helper had been watching the German observation balloon and its strange movements. When they reached the high knoll they, too, stopped to see if this might mean signaling to the enemy. The American driver's helper was a *poilu* who had been wounded at the first battle of the Marne in 1914 and long experience in the ways of the Huns had taught him to be suspicious of everything unusual. He knew that the means of communication between a captive balloon and the divisional commander was by telephone and such signaling as this must be to those that a wire could not reach. In broken English he shouted excitedly:

"Behold! Zat ess eet, in ze booshes zere, over ze field! Puff, puff, puff; behold! We have heem, *m'sieu'!* An' we capture heem now purty queek; right off, eh?"

The Yank was about to send the car forward again when his companion stopped him with another exclamation which made it worth while pausing a moment longer for a better view.

"Ha, look! Zee balloon, eet seegnal ze enemy, *m'sieu'*! Ha, he come! He come queek; he go fast! Ha! Somesing doing now!" The Frenchman had caught this last expression from his American friend. "An' eet ees ze *Croix Rouge* car, ze other wan. He but young boy. An' he fire; ha, he too has—what you say? catched on to ze seegnalers. But, *m'sieu'*, will not they reseest heem?"

The two were on their feet now, gazing with all eyes, excited. So they remained for some time—the Yank with clenched fists, the *poilu* rubbing his hands together. Then, as if at a signal, they both dropped into their seats and the ambulance rushed again along the by-way. Half an hour later, with but one wounded man and a Red Cross driver, unhurt, sitting beside him, the army ambulance drew up to the evacuation hospital tent. In answer to the curt query of the Major, the driver excused himself for bringing in only one man.

"You see, sir, we thought it was no more than fair, after what they had both done— discovered those Heinies inside our lines signaling to the boche balloon and it signaling back to them. This fellow inside that got his must have landed on 'em first, afoot, and they did him up. Then the young chap, he went 'em one better and I never seen a prettier fight. We seen it from the little hill."

"Did the German spies get away?" asked the surgeon.

"Only one did, and I think he'll get stopped. They must have seen it from the woods. He made a run fer his car and jumped into it; it's the speediest thing ever, I reckon. He was out of sight quicker'n a scared cootie, going for the woods. But the kid he got the other one; the one, he says, that hit the pink-checked lad."

"How did he get him?"

"Shot him. Let him have it like Pete the Plugger would 'a' done. Yes, sir! The kid's car run right along to about fifty yards of the bushes where they was hid and the kid jumped out; right off they began shootin' at him and he pulls a gun out of his Red Cross car as calm and as deliberate as if he was after prairie chicken and knowed he was goin' to get 'em, and commenced shootin'. They skinned for their car and one of 'em gets in and gets her goin', but the other one he turns round to take another shot at the kid who was kneelin' down and lettin' 'em have it proper and the feller keels over and the one in the car he skids off. I reckon the kid he jest about filled that there car full of lead, but the feller he got away, though if he wasn't hurt it's a wonder!"

"The lad is sure one scrapper, eh?" The surgeon was much tickled and slapped his leg at the realistic narrative of the ambulancier.

"He is, Major; all of that!" continued the soldier. "For a kid, or fer a veteran, for that matter, he is some boy with a gun! And he showed pluck, too, when we got there. You see, we seen and heard them Hun gas shells comin' over—that there Hun balloon give the range, I reckon—and we heard the gongs, too, but we reckoned the kid, bein' so excited over the fight, didn't get on to it, so the only thing to do was to get there right quick and you bet we did! Here was this one dead Hun with the Red Cross on his sleeve—the feller that the kid shot—and in the bushes was the kid bendin' over the feller what them Huns had knocked in the head, and the gas from two busted shells a sneakin' up on 'em lively. We had on our masks and we started to grab him and get him away. He hadn't saw us ner heard us come and he turned round on me with a drawed pistol, so's I thought it was all off sure. But the kid knowed us and didn't shoot. We yelled 'gas' at him and what did he do? Run to his car off there and get his mask? Never a bit of it! He jest sez to us: 'help me with this feller to my car,' he sez. 'I've got two masks there, his'n and mine' he sez. So I sez: 'this way's quicker; make tracks fer our car, young feller!' and I picked up the insensible feller and run with him to our car and the kid follered, and we got away from the gas. The kid he begged us to get here quick, or his pal might die and so that's why we come back with only one."

"Well, all right; excused, of course," said the Major.

"Now we're off, back up there, Major, and we'll try to make up fer—"

"It isn't lost time, or it wouldn't be if we could save that lad's life. Well, anyway—but you'd better wait a moment and I'll get the kid, as you call him—Richards—to go back with you and get his car."

The chief entered the tent and wended his way quickly down the long aisle, between

the rows of brown cots, many of which held
wounded men, he stopped here and there
for a word of encouragement, of advice,
or to answer a question. Reaching the farther
end he stood for a moment, looking down at a
white-faced figure lying very inert beneath
the blanket and at another sitting, with his
face in his hands, beside the cot. A woman
nurse, rather young, with wonderfully gentle
eyes, passed softly and whispered to the
Major.

"He feels it terribly; we don't often see
such grief, though he is not of the loud
weeping kind."

The Major nodded and, stooping forward,
laid his hand on the shoulder of the figure
in the chair.

"Come, Richards. No use sitting here;
there is much to do; much. Getting away
on duty will make you feel better."

Don looked up with a face that was drawn
with sorrow.

"But, Doctor, suppose he comes to and
asks for me? You are sure that he can't
get well?"

The doctor assented by a nod. "He cannot
recover," was his brief remark, uttered more
feelingly than usual with this man of long,

hard experience. Then he added with his usual attention to duty on his mind:

"He may become conscious later on. I'll let you know. After you get your car and bring in the next bunch you must run down to your base and report. They must assign you another helper. I have sent your description of the German signal man to headquarters and to the P. C. at the front of the woods section—I think they'll get him. And I'll send a note by you, telling what good work you did."

With the idea uppermost that it was his first duty to play the part of a good soldier in the work he had enlisted to do, Don got up to join the army ambulance. Two hours later, in his own car and at its best speed, he was returning from the Red Cross base. The man beside him began to think himself most unlucky to have been assigned to duty with this dare-devil of a driver, who spoke hardly a word and seemed not to care if they were presently piled in a heap and both killed. Around, past and in between lorries, trucks, ambulances, big guns being hauled to the front and marching men they dashed. When the evacuation hospital was again reached the young driver left the car with but a word to the new man, requesting him to wait, and was gone a long half hour.

"He has aked for you," said the nurse to Don. "His mind seems to be clear and he is not suffering, but the shock was too great. It has caused some immediate heart trouble and with the loss of blood—the Major can explain. Go right over and speak to the poor boy."

Don did so, almost in despair, but he was determined not to show it. Billy must get well; if there was anything in his thinking so, then he must be given every chance. And so Don met his pal with a smile.

"Hello, Billy! Feeling better? Soon be all right, I—"

"No, no! Don, the—nurse told me all about it; what you did and what you did for me, too. Don—we—we have only known each other—how long, Don?"

"Why, three whole days, Billy. But we'll know each other al—"

"Listen, Don. I know. Don't try to fool me. No use. West—I'm going—West. Pretty soon, too. A message, to my father and mother and brother, Don. Will you write it? I got the nurse to write this to introduce you to them, and to bid them good-bye. Then I only want you to write him a letter about me—a little. Can you tell them, Don, that I was not a coward— that I was not very much afraid—that I tried to do my duty? Don't tell them a lie— but—but if you could truthfully say something like that it will please them. Do you understand?"

Don could not trust his voice, but he nodded his head with very evident determination and, unlike anything he had ever done before, placed his hand over that of Billy's and held it. It was not a boylike act, but it seemed as though they were no longer boys, but creatures of profound and heart-stirring sentiment. The soft, droning voice of the dying youth ceased a little; then began again with halting, sometimes difficult speech.

"Father will be pleased, Don, and I know he will do as I request. But you are not to open and read the note the nurse wrote for me. You told me, Don—it was the first day—that you would like to go to college when you get through Prep, but that your father could never afford it with so many other boys to raise and educate. But if someone who cared a lot for you, compelled you to accept the money, then you would, Don, wouldn't you? Please, please, say yes, Don—if we have been friends. That's good—good. Tell me, Don—what school do you go to—now—when—you go—at home?"

"Brighton." Don just managed to pronounce the word.

"Don! Brighton! Oh—you didn't tell me that before. Brighton—was my school, too, Don. Class of—1915. and you—Don— too! Well—the good old school will have reason to be proud—of you!"

"Of you—of you, Billy!"

"Perhaps so, if—if I could have—lived— gone on doing things—tried to be—Don, ask the nurse to come here—or the—Major. I guess—I guess—"

The boy's face had suddenly grown whiter, if that were possible, and a deathly pallor came over it. Don went quickly to do as Billy asked. The nurse came to the bedside of the young man. She bent over him for what seemed a long while—a minute or more. Then she turned to Don.

"Going," she said. "He called your name again. Perhaps he can hear you." The nurse made way.

"Billy, dear Billy, I—I'm here," Don said, his lips close to his pal's ear. A faint smile came over the patient's face and then it became rigid. With a light heart Billy Mearns "went West."

CHAPTER XII

Tim

DON RICHARDS' new helper on the Red Cross ambulance was an undersized, red-headed Irishman by the name of Tim Casey. He was a month or two short of nineteen winters and, as he expressed it, an undetermined number of summers, but judging by the bleached-out color of his hair, which he assured Don was originally as black as a nigger's pocket, there must have been a long siege of sunny months. County Kerry was his birthplace and his native village was noted for its big men, his own father being almost a walking church steeple and his numerous brothers all six-footers. Tim was the only short one— "the runt in the litter," he called himself.

"But if yez are proper anxious to know an' ye look loike ye couldn't survive the day out wid not knowin' all o' me fam'ly histhry, Oi'll tell yez this: Phw'at was left out o' me body was put in me head, do yez moind? for by the holy Saint Macherel, Oi'm the

smartest o' the bunch. Me faither's poorer
than whin he was born, an' me brithers
couldn't foind pennies if they growed on the
grass. But me? Faith, if wan o' these here
boche zizzers don't have me name wrote on
it, thin whin the war's over Oi'm goin' to
America an' make a million pounds, loike
me friend Mike McCarty did!"

"Good for you! That's nearly five million
dollars. Hope you get it," said Don.

"Thanks. Could yez lend me phw'at they
call two francs, now, to git us both some
sweet, brown, mushy things, loike candy,
but diff'runt? It's me own treat, now."

"Chocolate? Sure. Here you are. You
can get them at the Y. M. C. A. hut in an
abri back of the woods and near our dressing
station," Don informed him, and a little
later the two lads were enjoying mouthfuls
of very satisfying sweetness, as they waited
for more wounded to be brought out to them.
And as they waited Don turned to a sentry
to ask some questions. The sentry was
glad to impart:

"The P. C. came over a little while ago
and I heard him tell the medical sergeant,
here in the doorway, that they had a message
from the evacuation hospital about a Hun in

a Red Cross ambulance getting away around
the woods here. The man I relieved said he
saw the fellow go past, and he went a whizzing,
but he didn't question him; nobody does
anything with the Red Cross on it. The
P. C. said that they hadn't seen hide nor
hair of the man, nor the ambulance, since
and they think he must have been heading
for another sector. He can rip off his red
crosses there and let on he's something else
important. They do those stunts. But if
he's caught, it's good-night for him!"

Don was keenly disappointed. He had sent
some very well directed bullets straight after
the escaping car, but they must have hit
the sides at an angle and glanced off. However cold-blooded and murderous it appeared
thus to shoot down a man, even a declared
and vicious enemy, the boy had done this
deed against one who had murdered his dear
pal, Billy Mearns. Moreover, Don had wanted
to write to his father and to Mr. Stapley,
at home, that the escaped man who had
helped to blow up the mills had been discovered and accounted for. Don felt sure
that this fake Red Cross driver and spy
was the same man—the narrow-eyed, tall
individual that he and Clem Stapley had spot-

ted and listened to on the train coming from Brighton, more than three months ago.

Now that the German spy had escaped again, he would surely turn up somewhere else and do more harm. Like his bearded confederate at Lofton, he could probably speak English and American English perfectly, and no doubt he knew French also, for these spies were of that sort—sharp-witted, brainy, learned scoundrels!

"He will try, yes, no doubt, but it will amount to very little. What can he do?" replied the sentinel to whom Don made his pessimistic remark.

"Are yez on to this?" said Tim Casey. "The Limburgers are a very smart bunch, yis; in many ways, yiz; but, me b'y, they're awful stupid, do yez see? These here Huns are loike parrots. They're windy imitators, ye see, but bad 'cess to thim, they got no real sense. They don't know just phw'at they want. A parrot, me b'y, is always hollerin' fer a cracker, but did yez iver see it eat wan? Ye did not."

"By which you mean to say—" began Don.

"Thot the dumb Dutch will do somethin' crazy sooner er later an' hang hisself. They jist natchally go round with a rope ready.

8

An' look phw'at they're doin' in this war. Preparin' the thickest koind of a rope an' makin' it good an' tight around their fool necks be desthroyin' iv'rything they come acrost so that whin they have t' pay they can't do it!''

It might seem to one not familiar with the risks of battle that the work of an army or Red Cross ambulance driver must have been intolerably monotonous. But such an idea is very far from the truth. No two journeys afield were alike and so varied was the work an so soul-stirring the sights and sounds of two great armies facing each other, with bared fangs, that the part of any kind of an actor in the war become a terribly real experience.

There was no monotony in this thing for Don Richards, nor doubtless, for any other ambulance driver in France during the great war, and our hero could affirm this, especially when a shell, making a direct hit, carried away all the latter part of his ambulance and burst on the ground beyond, not forty feet away. Tim and Don were dragged one way by the impact, a hundredth of a second later tossed, in a heap in the other direction clear of motor and front wheels, upon a friendly bit of mud and left to wonder whether the world had come to an end completely, or was only just beginning to. And yet the boys came through without a scratch worth mentioning.

Tim Casey worried Don not a little in always being slow with his gas mask. The boy told his helper that it would serve him right some time if he got a sore throat from the gas. But the Irishman laughed; he was really not afraid of anything normal, and abnormal things he treated with a sort of lenient bluff, cursing them soundly in his soft Irish brogue and dodging them because it was the habit to do so.

"The sthinkin' stuff is as vile as the dirthy Huns thot sind it over, an' if Oi had the villain thot invinted it Oi'd maul the face off him, I wud!"

"But suppose he were a big fellow, like some of these Huns are?" Don asked in jest, to tease his companion.

"Big er little, it don't matter," replied Tim. "It ain't the soize of a mon thot counts; it's the spirit of him," which Don was glad to admit. And he sized up the little Irishman as one having a large spirit when it came to a scrap.

And there was the movement of men, of guns big and little, of airplanes; there were aerial battles, bombings, raids and counter-attacks, which were seen but little by the ambulance drivers, but the immediate results were realistic enough. Tim Casey found a remark or two that fitted every occasion and he declared one fight even bloodier than an Irish holiday.

"Ah, me b'y, if the bloody gobs in this here scrap had only had clubs—shillalahs—phw'at wud they done to each ither? If Oi was the ginral of this outfit, b'gorry, Oi'd sthart out a raidin' party of all Irish from County Kerry, give 'em shillalahs an' the war'd be over the next day! The kaiser wud call it inhuman, of coorse, an' right he'd be, but we'd win jist the same."

"Now, what could clubs do against guns?" Don laughed. "They's have you all shot dead before you got near enough to soak them."

"An' wud they? Thin, me b'y, how come they to use bayonets? Tell me thot."

"It's a thing I can't understand and I guess I never will; unless it's after the ammunition on both sides gives out that they use them. Maybe if they'd do away with

ammunition in wars shillalahs would be
handier than guns and worse than bayonets."

"Oi'll write the C. and C. about thot
same," said Tim.

But whatever frightful atrocities and science
had done to make this war a horror beyond
the conception of those who could not witness
it, the most terrible of all was the Hun
bombing of hospitals. There was, as with
many other things indulged in by the Germans, nothing gained by these acts—nothing
but deeper exasperation and determination
on the part of those who were forced to fight
the Hun. He saw others through his own
shade of yellow and imagined that he could
frighten his foes and lessen their morale
that way—but it produced exactly the opposite effect.

The cross-roads evacuation hospital tents
back of the Montdidier front suffered from
German airmen, not many days after the
great German push for Amiens had been
stopped. Plainly an act of hatred, this
bombing gained nothing for the Huns. They
had lost thousands of men in killed, wounded
and prisoners and wanted the Allies to suffer
still more.

Don and Tim had received but one wounded

man from the dressing station back of the woods on the hill. Looking for additional wounded, who might be struggling in, they had run around the northern edge of the woods and a half-mile farther on, near the front line trenches, when a military police-man rode out from an old orchard and stopped them.

"Too much noise from that motor of yours and the Heinies are very wide awake," he said. "They'll spot you and be pretty likely to get you.

"We had'nt seen any Hun fliers and we thought they might be generally keeping quiet," Don said.

"They are quiet just now, but I reckon it's just before a storm," said the M. P. "That's the way it usually is. If they sud-denly start to put down a barrage before a drive or a raid you'll be in for it. You know a good many of the bullets fly high and pretty nearly half of them ricochet. You fellows can't get back of a tree as I and my horse can. Better go back."

Tim, who was driving the car, having now become rather proficient at it, had a word to say, as usual.

"R-right you are, me b'y! We was jist

calculatin' if they sint some whizzers over
to ketch 'em in these here dish pans; do ye
see?" And Tim tapped his helmet. "We're
lookin' fer sowineers, we are."

"Oh, yes, you'd stop 'em! If a 122-shell
would be coming right for that topknot
of yours it would veer off and go on, hoping
to draw blood where none was already
flowing."

"Faith, an' how did yez iver git in the sarv-
ice? Ye're color blind; me mither dyed me
hair blue; can't ye see it? to offset me too
cheerful disposition."

"If you told me it was green I might
believe you. But on the top of the green
it's all rufus, Mike, all rufus."

"Well, misther bobby, it's all right fer
yez. But it's a fightin' color; ain't it?"

"I believe that! But come now, lads;
you'd better beat it while your skins are
whole."

Tim began turning the car. "Sure an'
ye loike t' give orders. An' Oi'll be tellin'
yez this; if a shell comes your way an' mixes
wid yer anatomy, er yez git overcome wid
hard wor-r-rk settin' on thot plug all day
ye'll be hopeful glad t' see us comin'. So
long!"

Not many minutes later the boys reached
the hospital and out came the Major in his
long, white blouse. When the *brancardiers*
had carried the wounded man into the X-ray
tent, the chief had a word to say to the
ambulanciers gathered by the roadside.

"Hold yourselves in readiness, boys; we
have orders to evacuate at once; get every
man that we can let go out of here and be
ready to pull up stakes at a moment's notice.
That'll be if the Germans succeed in advancing. It is believed they are getting ready
to make another push. So, as soon as we
list our cases fully as to condition and treat-
ment, in half an hour's time, we shall ask
you to go get busy. You had better line up
along the road. Those cases in the first
three cars you will report and they'll go on
through to the convalescent bases, as ordered
by the Red Cross commission assistant;
the others will go to the nearest Red Cross
base. Now, then, stand ready boys, and
tune up your motors till we call on you for
the stretcher work. We haven't enough
brancardiers to do it quickly." The Major
re-entered the tent.

Don turned to a fellow-driver and was
making a remark when Tim pulled his sleeve.

"Do yez hear thot coffee grinder comin'?"

From a distance there was the hum of a motor high in air. As it grew louder, it was easily recognized as a double motor—the unmistakable sound, never in tune, that giant twin propellers make.

"Sounds like a bombing plane. Ours or the Huns'?" queried a driver, gazing aloft. The bunch were all doing that now, as a matter of habit. One chap was squinting through a field glass.

"There she comes out of that cloud! Pretty high up. Say, it's a Heinie! What's he up to? Guns can't reach him at that elevation, but *his* bombs can reach the earth."

"Going to worry them reserves, I reckon. Where's the Frog-eaters? They'll chase him home if they go up."

There seemed to be no French birdmen around and the German was evidently taking advantage of this. He was coming on straight over the hospital and lessening his height every second. In thirty seconds he had come down to half the distance from the earth and began to sweep about in a circle, or like a gigantic figure eight, much as a great, bloodthirsty hawk does when scanning the earth below for its prey.

Suddenly, from beneath the airplane the watchers saw something long and gray which seemed to poise a moment under the airplane, then drop and gain momentum every fraction of a second, and fall like a plummet straight for the hospital tent. The watchers, all experienced, knew well what it was, but any cry of warning was lost in the explosion that followed not a hundred feet beyond the tent.

"The dirty spalpeen!" Don heard Tim shout. "Come down here wanst an' thin do it! Gin'ral,"—Tim insisted upon calling Don that—"he'll make surer the next time! Come, there's wor-rk inside!"

There was. Don caught a glimpse of two *ambulanciers* diving under their cars, of another running somewhere else, evidently for shelter. The boy's ears welcomed the sharp crack, crack of field pieces and he knew the anti-aircraft were demonstrating their readiness. He got one more glimpse of the Hun plane over the roof of the tent and saw another gray thing descending. Then he was inside.

When Don had looked in not two hours before he noted that at least three-fourths of the cots were occupied, the convalescents walking slowly about, or seated in little groups, talking; the nurses were busily engaged. The sad sounds pervading the place were horribly depressing to him. He could not long endure the labored breathing of those who were passing over the Great Divide, the persistent coughing of the severely gassed, the sight of shell-shocked men, who, without a scratch, cowered and stared about like crazy people, the moaning of those who suffered and the smell of anesthetics.

But now all was changed. The scene was beyond description. Don was awake to his duty and eager for it. There must be strong wills and hands to aid and reassure these helpless fellows. The doctors and nurses, frightened but heroic, could not do it all.

With a sound like the rending of a thousand taut cords a hole was torn in the tent roof, the interior was filled with streaks of flame and smoke and flying objects, a choking odor filled the air with stinging fumes and through it all came groans, screams and curses in a hideous meledy. Wounded men some with limbs in splints, some half covered with bandages, leaped or tumbled out of their cots, and sought imagined shelter anywhere. Some limped or crawled outside.

Some lay still and prayed aloud. Another
bomb fell that was a second clean miss of
the main tent, though it struck the corner
of the medical supplies tent and scattered
the Major's personal effects beyond recovery.
Two other bombs came down in quick suc-
cession, one in the road beyond, cutting a
hind tire, lifting the top off of the last ambulance in the line and knocking down two
sentries. The fifth bomb went wild and did
no harm. Those who still had their eyes
on the murderous thing aloft saw it turn
eastward and rise beyond the reach of the
guns.

There was much work of a very serious
nature during the next few hours and then
a night of running back and forth. The
first streaks of a murky dawn witnessed the
evacuation hospital nearly empty and ready
for new cases. Two lads in a rain-soaked
and mud-bespattered ambulance, carrying
a cheerful soldier whose only need was a
week of rest, stopped by the roadside on the
way to Paris—and, with their passenger's
consent, rolled up in blankets on floor and
seat to sleep the sleep of the just fagged.

CHAPTER XIII

Wash

MY boy, I want to commend you, for your aid when they bombed us last week. Haven't had a chance to before. If all of the fellows had been as cool and as helpful as you and that little, red-headed Irishman we would have had less trouble straightening things out. I see he is running his own car now. Who is your helper?" So spoke Major Little, when he came out of the operating room to get a breath of fresh air, and said Don.

"I guess I'll get a colored chap, if I get any," the boy replied. "A lot of new cars have come over and they want men. I can get along alone. Some of the fellows do."

"Better to have company. Helps the *morale*. Gives a chance of aid if one fellow gets hit. Better all round. It is the policy of the service; but we can't always get what we want."

"Glad you didn't have to move after all, Doctor."

"No, but the expectation now is that the move will come farther north—against the British. Or it may be to the south. If so, some of you fellows will have to be transferred to that sector and it will give us a little rest here.

"I guess you won't be sorry, sir. You have worked hard."

"Yes, pretty hard—right along. We of the Medical Department and of the Red Cross got into it before our fighters did. But the time has come now."

"I'd like to see some of our boys get busy in a big way. I wish I could have joined the army."

"Your work is fully as important—and daring—and useful. And, remember this, it is far more humane. You've no right to feel dissatisfied."

"I'm not, Major—not a bit of it. You may count on me! Are there any more *blessés* to go down now?"

The Americans had begun to take part in the fighting. They had begun to do things in a small way, but this seemed to cause very little stir in France, except among those who had knowledge of the sterling character of the boys from the United States.

The French commonly knew nothing actually. They saw nothing to make them think they were any more than a staunch-looking lot of fellows, many of whom needed a lot of drilling in modern warfare before they could hope to turn the tide of battle. There had been little evidence, so far, of this aid materializing, and even the most optimistic *poilus* had begun to doubt and to question. They had become a trifle fed up on American promises and they now wondered if the Yanks really meant to fight in a large way, or had come over only to skirmish and to bolster up the courage of the Allies by remaining in reserve.

True, the Americans had done a little commendable fighting, aided by the British and the French. Brigaded with the "Tommies" they had taken some hard knocks above Amiens. Brigaded with the French they had helped hold the Germans around Montdidier, but what could they do on a large scale that would really count? Were they actually going to be a factor in war?

Well, these questions were to be answered shortly, but would the result allay all doubt in the minds of all the anxious ones? The Americans were arriving upon the field of

battle in rapidly increasing numbers. They
had come across three thousand miles of
water in spite of the German submarines.
Was it like those vigorous inhabitants of
the greatest country on earth, to hold back
now in the great contest?

Spring had arrived. It was past the middle
of April. The grass was newly green. The
fruit trees were coming into blossom and the
foliage was beginning to bud. The birds were
singing everywhere, even amidst the desolate
scenes of battle. Except where the shells
and shrapnel of the opposing armies had
torn the ground and battered the forests,
there was the peacefulness over all and
beauty of the new life of the season. Even
now not far back from the fighting front
of the Allies, some daring tillers of the soil
were making ready to plant their crops.

But alternating with the days of balmy
stillness came the rains—days and days
when the whole face of nature was like a
vast mop, soaked to fullness, dripping and
cold. And when it rained it did nothing
but rain. It had become almost an icy drizzle
on the twentieth and the soldiers in the
trenches, those bivouacking in the open
and the homeless refugees who had fled

before the German advance, were corre-
spondingly miserable. It was, as in the winter
months, a time for greatcoats, dry footwear,
if such were possible, and the making of
fires wherever fuel was to be had.

Don Richards was ready with every handy
means to meet the intolerable weather con-
ditions, and his new helper, Washington
White, the blackest darky and one of the
best natured that ever exposed a wide row
of ivories. Washington fairly hugged himself because luck had thrown him in with
a lad who had camped and roughed it through
wild country and knew nearly every trick
of out-of-door life, from vacation experiences
with his Boy Scout troop, and from camping
out with the Brighton biology class.

"Wha—wha—what we gwine tuh du now,
Mist' Donal'? Ain't a-gwine tuh stay yer; is
we? In all dis slop o' mud?"

"Just that!" Don replied. "No more
mud here than everywhere else. I guess the
whole world is one big puddle by the way
things look, except perhaps the Desert of
Sahara or the American bad lands. This
is as good a spot to put up in for the night
as anywhere that I know of—in this part
of the earth, anyhow."

9

"But wha's de matter wif gwine on back tuh de hospital?"

"No place there. You know they've asked us to give up our quarters for a while to some new nurses just come over, and we've got to be polite to the ladies. The orders have been all along that if we were empty and night shut down on us on the road, to bunk anywhere and go on in the morning, with that much time gained. Every minute counts these days. Get the matches under the seat there, will you? And there's a bottle of coal-oil wrapped in a rag by the tool box. Reach down that camp hatchet."

"But, lawsee, Mist' Donal', we'd be somewhar's en' a roof en' have lights en' a wahm meal—"

"Say, forget it! Haven't we got the roof of the car? And haven't we got a light," pointing to the one lighted lamp of the car, "and as for a warm meal—oh, boy! I'll make you think you're at the Waldorf-Astoria when I get to frying this good old American bacon and these French eggs. You ought to be doing it, really, but the next time'll be your turn. Now then, chase around for some wood!"

"B-r-r-r! Dis road's awful dahk en' de

wood'll be all wet's a wet hen, en' say, Mist'
Donal', wid all dem sojers kickin' de bucket
back yondah en' off dere in dem trenches
en' de amberlances chasin' back en' fo'th
wid deaders—say, lawsee, Ah's plum scairt
'bout projectin' roun' dis—"

"Aw, go on, you superstitious simp!
The wood won't be wet inside if it isn't
rotten. Don't be a coward. Why, boy,
you tell me you're not going to be afraid
of bullets and shells and bombs and gas.
Aren't they worse than people already dead?
You make me tired. Go chase—!"

"But shells is jes' shells en' bullets is jes'
bullets en' all dat, but dese yere deaders
may be ghos'ses. Lawsee, man! Ef one o'
dem t'ings 'd rise up en' grab yo'—ooh!"

"Say, you weren't cut out for this kind
of work, Wash. What are you going to do
when we've got to haul some dead people,
or when some poor chap dies on the way
in? I've had three do that with me so far
and it may happen right along. See here,
if you want to stay with me you've got to
be sensible and brave. There's no such
thing as ghosts and the only thing about
a dead person is that it's awful to think
they've had to be killed. Are you going
after—?"

"Yes, suh; yes, suh! Ah'll git de wood, ef dere is any. Ah reckon Ah ain't so much scairt as Ah let on! Ah reckon Ah ain't."

"You'd better not be scared at anything if you want to stay with this outfit. This is no coward's job, Washington. And say, with that name of yours, now, you oughtn't to be afraid of the whole German army, even if they were all dead. George Washington wasn't afraid of anything. Is your first name George?"

"Ah reckon 'tis, but Ah doan' know fo' shuah. Mah mammy allus jes' call me Wash er Washington. No, suh, dat man Ah's name fo' wasn't no coward. Ah'll git de wood, but Ah'll take de hatchet."

But Wash had become more reconciled to a camp in a soggy field by the time he had set his teeth into the bacon, several boxes of which, with other good things, filled a grub box in the car. Then, warmed by a fire that roared in spite of the drizzling rain and mist, and later rolled in a thick army blanket on the bottom of the ambulance, the darky's snores soon gave evidence that ghosts were haunting him no longer.

The morning dawned with lifting mists and a breeze that was making a counterdrive to chase away the enemy clouds in order to let the peaceful sunlight through. Don, while lighting the fire, planning the breakfast and prodding Wash to get up and cook it, felt much better for the change.

"Hump yourself, you lazy snorefest you, and just look at the battle going on out here!"

That had the effect of hastily arousing Wash. Not even the promise of a crap game is dearer to one of his kind than a scrap of this sort.

"Whar-whar's de fight? Ah doan' heah no shootin'!"

"See those Hun clouds?" enthused Don. "Well, that west wind comes straight from good old America and it's making the boches hustle."

"Lawsee! Ah reckon you-all's done got 'em! Wha-whar's dat bacon en' dem aigs. Yo' jes' watch me git up one breakfas' dat'll fetch roun' yo' senses! Golly! Heah dat?"

They both heard. A rumbling noise coming rapidly nearer along the road. Wash thought it might be the Germans, but Don assured him that was impossible. The Americans were on the job now. There was further evidence of this at hand, for out of the dispelling mists came a yellow touring car closely followed by a gigantic khaki-colored lorry, or camion. Right back of that another and another, and more, and still more until the road was filled, farther than the eye could see, with the steadily moving line. Each big vehicle was filled with soldiers.

Don had seen a crest on the leading touring car. He knew this bunch of men, for it had been whispered from mouth to mouth at the Red Cross base hospital that the marines were on their way from westward training camps.

"Our engineers up there with General Carney showed the Huns what kind of stuff the Americans are made of," one official had said. "Trust the marines for driving that down the Germans throats—when they get at it!"

That was it: when they got at it. But when were they to get at it? Was French official red tape in the way, or was it that the British and French generals feared to trust the untried Americans too far? Must a desperate need arise to make an actual test of the Americans?

The boys stood by their car, waving their hats at the men in passing, and many a wave of arms they got back. Many a good-natured jibe was exchanged between the lorries and the ambulance.

"Hurrah! Go to it, you blood drinkers!" shouted Don.

"That's the stuff, buddy! It's sauerkraut in Berlin for us before we're done!"

"We're goin' to give Fritzy fits!" roared another marine.

"How do you like cruising on land?" asked Don of another carload.

"Can't see much difference between this country now and the good, old ocean!" was the rejoinder.

"One's as wet as the other!"

"An' ye can't drink either of 'em!" shouted a third.

"Oh, look at the coon!" called a private in another camion.

"Say, nig, lost; ain't yu? I reckon yu ol' mammy's jes' cryin' huh eyes out fo' huh little Alabama coon!"

"Huh! Ah reckon yu-all frum down Souf, too; eh, soljah man?" yelled Wash.

"I am that! Georgia! But everything goes just the same over here!"

"Say, a darky! Wonder these Frog-eaters haven't got him in a cage! rarity over here!" The fourth camion contigent were impressed.

"Well, I bet our Red Cross friend there has to eat his share of hog fat and hoe cake!"

This went on for a good three-quarters of an hour until the last lorry had passed. Then the lads turned to a hasty breakfast.

"They're the marines, Wash; the Fifth and Sixth Regiments. You know they have a slogan in the Navy: 'a marine never retreats'."

"In de Navy. What dem sojahs doin' in de Navy?"

"They're the soldiers attached to battle-ships. They fight on land when needed, and I guess they're going to be needed here!"

"Did yu-all know enny of 'em pussonel, Mist' Donal'? Ah seed yo' lookin' lak yo' was gwine ter call a feller in one o' de las' cars be name, en' he look at yo' so't o' queeah, too."

"Yes, I happen to know one of them, Wash. You are some observer. He's a chap from my home town. His name's Clement Stapley. He joined the marines before I left home. But I hardly think he knew me, Wash."

"Yes, Ah t'ink he done knowed yo', frum de look awn his face. But mebbe he wa'n't quite shuah. Why'n't yu-all holler at him en' pass de time o' day an' yell how he is?"

"Oh, well, you see, we were not such very good friends, and I was afraid he might still feel sore at me. Maybe I'll get a chance to see him again. Well, come on; we've got to be going. There's a lot of work ahead."

CHAPTER XIV

SHIFTED

THE battle sector southeast of Amiens and around Mondidier became quiet during the latter part of April and early May, and, true to Major Little's predictions, he and the force under him had not much to do. There was still some local fighting. It would not be modern warfare without. Each side sought almost constantly to harass the other and to impress its enemy with its power and readiness. Still, there were a few casualties, so that the dressing stations, and operating room in the evacuation hospital were not idle, and a few ambulances were making almost continuous trips up and down the well-traveled highway.

Not far back of the road from Paris to Amiens the newly-begun American graveyard, with its regular cross-headboards, had grown somewhat. Its mounds were often decorated with roses, field poppies and wild flowers laid on them by the tenderhearted natives, mostly children. It was such sights,

(138)

together with those of the ruined homes
and shell-torn cities within reach of the
German guns, that made the beholder pause
and wonder how it was that humankind
could permit war and its horrors.

The so-called second German drive of 1918
had been launched along the river Lys
against Ypres and toward the Channel ports
in early April. But it had proved a failure.
The firm stand of the British wore out and
finally stopped the Huns. Then, more and
more furious at these repeated checks, the
German High Command, with Hindenburg
and Ludendorff at the head, shifted their
offensive toward the south. If the British
lion could not be separated from his ally,
the French eagle, and slain at once then
perhaps a supreme effort would gain the
road to Paris. The threatened destruction
of that city would surely bring victory to
Germany and thus enable the kaiser to
impose "peace at any price" upon the Allies.

Therefore, on the last day of April began
the strengthening of the German line from
Noyon to Rheims and a consequent push
around Noyon. But the Huns made no
progress and once more gnashed their teeth
in preparation for a desperate onslaught.

It was planned that this should break through
at the long coveted points nearest their
first objective, the city of Paris.

Just as the storm broke along the Oise
and the Marne rivers, there came a surprise
to the British, French and Germans. To
the Huns it was like a thunderbolt out of a
clear sky.

The Americans, under French direction,
backed by French artillery, went over the
top from hastily dug trenches, and made a
counter-attack at Cantigny, which threw the
enemy back nearly a mile. The Yanks, at
the end of May, still held their positions,
against the Huns most violent attacks.

Coming up the Paris-Amiens road on a
bright morning—the first day of June—Don
and Wash, carrying additional supplies for
the dressing stations back of Cantigny, met
a long line of yellow American lorries—no
new thing now, but fraught with deep sig-
nificance.

"The marines again, Wash—our marines—
going south. I bet they're ordered into the
fight. You heard what the assistant to our
commissioner said to Surgeon-Major Brown:
'There's likely to be some hard work stopping
the Heinies on the road out there east of

Paris'—the road" Don explained, the Major
said "to a place they call Rheims. The
Huns have got as far as the river Marne,
and that's where they were in 1914. But
I'll bet they don't get much farther—not if
our boys are going into it!"

"Is dey enny cullud sojahs in de fight?"
asked Wash.

"I guess not right at this place, but I
think there are, somewhere along the line.
Someone told me so—a regiment or more
of them."

"Well, den, what dey wants tuh do is
jes' give 'em some razzors 'en say tu 'em:
'Look-a-yer, yo' niggahs, dese yer Germans
ain't no real while folks—dat is real qual'ty—
dey is jes' po' whites 'en no 'count 'en dey
hates niggahs. Now den, go in 'en carve
'em up!' Sho, man, dey wouldn't be no
German army in 'bout fo' minutes."

"Why, that's right, Wash! Great idea!
I'm going to see General Pershing about
that. Or, say, how would it do to tell those
colored soldiers that every Heinie's a brother
to a 'possum, or that a great big flock of fat
chickens is roosting low over in the German
trenches! Wouldn't they drop down on those
Huns and scare 'em to death?"

"Aw, gwan, you's kiddin' me, yo' is! Say, ain't we gwine tuh stop somewhar's 'en see dese marines go by an' holler at 'em lak we done—?"

"No, indeed. We've got to go on and get back," said Don. "Orders are to report near LaFerté, to a French officer. The evacuation hospitals down there are all French, I guess. And now all the army down there is French, too, I expect, so we'll bring in their wounded mostly. But if our boys—"

"Does dese yer Frenchers all yell an' hollah when dey's hurt bad?" Wash asked. So far he had seen but two of them, both seriously wounded, and they had done a good deal of groaning and calling for water. But the question went unanswered, for just at the moment the ambulance was compelled to veer off nearly into the ditch in order to dodge a broken-down car and the ever passing lorries, the negro being bounced almost off his seat.

"Ah doan keer whar we goes tu from yere, jes' so's we git somewhar's whar de sun shines lak hit do now fo' a little while. Ah suttenly doan lak dis puddle bizness what we has mos' de time sense Ah ben in dis

yere France. Hit sure am some wet country.
Now dis day ain' so bad, so Ah'll jes' tap
wood—" and he rapped himself on the
head.

The round trip completed, Don and Wash
at the base hospital, re-stocked their car
for any emergency. They started out on
a new road, coming up with the tail end
of the marines in their big camions—passing
them, one by one. The way led east, then
south and east again, passing first through
the town of Senlis, then around the little
city of Meaux, then away on a splendid
road toward Rheims. Before reaching the
objective beyond the town of LaFerté, the
road crossed the beautiful Marne, called a
river, though Don regarded it merely a
big creek, as it would be called in America.

Oh and ever on, rumbled the camions,
the yellow lorries with the marines, and
Don expected again to catch sight of Clem
Stapley. However, it was not these fighting
men that most interested him, for on this
Rheims road the boy saw for the first time
what he would probably never see again—
refugees, fleeing from the German army.

It was a sight never to be forgotten—one
to wring pity out of the most stony-hearted,

to sober the most waggish, to sadden the
gentler-minded as hardly even death, or
the suffering of the wounded could do.
Driven from their homes, fearing the wrath
of the invader, expecting only to return and
find all their property destroyed, except
the little they could carry away, given
over to pillage, or the flames. They trudged
along, embittered by injustice, powerless to
protest, stolid or weeping, but all of one
mind. They sought only a place of safety
from the Huns. They were mostly afoot;
many old men, the younger and middle-
aged women and the stronger boys and
girls were the beasts of burden, carrying
or drawing great loads in makeshift carts,
or light wagons, the more fortunate having
horse or cow, or perhaps donkey or dog,
harnessed to help. On these loads rode
the smaller children and the very aged.

Even the soldiers, singing and laughing
as they went on to battle, some of them
to death or lifelong suffering, and as gay as
if nothing but a picnic lay before them,
ceased their music and raillery, when they
saw the first of these refugees.

The French medical officer at the evacuation
hospital near LaFerté spoke enough English

to make himself understood by the American
Red Cross ambulance drivers, half a dozen
of whom had reported to duty before Don
arrived on the scene. These fellows greeted
him exuberantly and all stood in a row ready
to receive orders.

"One of ze dressed staisheon ess more
veree far up ze road at zee feets of one hill,
m'sieu', Eet is maybe one kilo from zee enemy
at ze Château-Thierry. Go where eet is
and carry all ze wound' you can to bring
heem *par-ici*. Then we operate and dispose,
m'sieurs. Allons!"

The ambulances raced away in a string,
Don leading. Then began again the experiences of near approach to the battle line,
hearing the almost constant rattle of small
arms and the hardly less continuous roar
of larger guns, seeing the shattered buildings
and trees and shell-holes in the most un-
expected places. The military police were
on duty along the roads. Military messengers
were hurrying back and forth. *Brancardiers*
were crossing and re-crossing the fields, with
their stretchers empty or laden. Field artillery was moving forward to position. Troops
were going in to engage the enemy, or coming
out to rest and others waiting in reserve.

10

Ammunition carriers lugged forward their heavy loads. Food for the men in battle was being prepared in hastily set-up kitchens. Sometimes a shell exploded and punctuated the tremendous activity.

"Now then, Wash, mind your eye. We've got to get in where, any minute, we may run into a big bang and go up a mile high, or maybe get buried alive or dead under about a ton of earth. Here's where it is you've been saying you'd like to get—right in among the fighters. So be prepared for the worst!"

"Ah ain't ezakly ready fo' no sech carryin's on ez dis," the darky remarked, rolling his ivory eye-balls until Don thought the pupils would go out of sight and stay there. "How—how long we gotta stay yere an' what's de mattah wiv me jes' droppin' off 'bout dis place 'en waitin' twill yu-all gits back from in yondah? Kaint see how Ah's gwine be much use nohow."

"You stay right on this car!" ordered Don. "What did you come for? When you get hit, then it's time to talk about quitting. From your color I didn't believe you had a single streak of yellow in you."

Wash stared hard at Don for a moment.

A big, whizzing shell, with a noise like that made by a nail when thrown through the air, passed over, not very far away, and exploded with a horrible rending sound, but the negro only shook himself and then grinned. Presently he replied to his companion:

"An' Ah ain't yaller, neither! No, sah! En' yu-all ain't gwine tuh have no call tuh say Ah is yaller. No, sah! Ah's gwine tuh stay on dis job ontil de yearth jes' fade away an' kingdom come, Ah is. Scairt? Is Ah? Yu jes' watch me! An' ef Ah's gotta git hit, why Ah jes' gits hit an' Ah reckon Ah kin stan' it ez well ez a yuther o' them niggahs a-fightin', or any white man, either! Yes, sah!"

And that was all there was to it. Wash meant what he said. Not another whimper did Don hear from him, no matter what their duties were, nor how fast the shells flew. The darky was on the job to prove that he was all one solid color, figuratively as well as literally, even if his name was White. And it became certain that there was no pallor in his liver to indicate his name.

The boys' first trip close to the battle

lines near Château-Thierry resulted in their return with three Frenchmen, one dying and beyond possible help, and two others wounded. Don and Wash had reached the crest of a hill on the road running southwest into LaFerté when they came upon a Red Cross ambulance which had been disabled. Don pulled up a moment to ask if he could briefly give aid, thinking to tow the other car in, if necessary. It was not the custom for a car loaded with *blessés* to spend any time on the road, if it could be avoided.

A weazen little man, with a foreign face, replied to the boy, in good English:

"Can you lend us a heavy wrench? We have only one and a light one. We need two to take off a bolt."

Don produced the desired tool from his box and turned to hand it to the little fellow. At the same instant the voice of someone on the other side of the crippled car called quite loud and in French, presumably a command to the little man. The latter made answer as if in protest. Then he handed the wrench back to Don.

"We can obtain another. We should not keep you. Thanks."

"No, use it," Don insisted. "I must

give my wounded some water and see if
they are comfortable. It will not take you
long."

The little man ran quickly to his car
and dived beneath it. Don, influenced partly
by curiosity and partly by instinct, walked
past the front end and on to the other side
of the disabled car. A man there, whose
voice he had heard—glared at him for a
moment, then turned away, rounding the
rear end of the car and keeping his back to
Don. This fellow was tall, thin, with a narrow
face and contracted eyes. He was dressed
in khaki, with the white band and Red Cross
on his arm.

The boy stood pondering but a moment.
He knew where he had seen this man before
and under what circumstances. Evidently
Don also was recognized. Without a word
the youth retraced his steps. He knew
very well from what exact spot he could
draw his rifle and he knew also that Wash
knew how to handle a gun and that he would
glory in doing so where any kind of heroics
were to be pulled off.

CHAPTER XV

ON THE WAY

WASH, listen: You know how to use this. Magazine's full. You're to use it—just when I tell you, or maybe before. There's a chap around that's got to go along with us, Wash, and there's a cord in the tool-box to tie him with. Mind you don't shoot me! Lie low till I shout."

Don went back to the crippled car.

"Well, does it work? Got it out?" he asked of the little man and received a muffled reply from beneath the *chassis*. Don walked around the mudguard past the rear end, and looked along the other side. No one was in sight. Had the tall man slipped into the car? He would find out.

"Nice car you have here—don't see many as fine in the service," he remarked to the man beneath. Again a muffled reply. One can hardly give attention to needless questions and wrestle with a refractory bolt. "How is she fitted inside?" Don queried, putting one hand on the latch of the full-length doors and the other on the butt of his revolver in its holster. But the doors were fastened on the inside.

"Don't open those doors! Don't try to, for the love of God!" yelled the small man, from the ground and instantly his wrinkled face emerged, followed by his wiry little body. "We're loaded with explosives for mines and they'll go off. Keep away from it!" Whether this was true or not and whether the fellow really felt frightened or was pretending, he certainly assumed it well. Don involuntarily backed away from the car.

"Oh, but that was a narrow escape! We'd all be sky-high if—" he began again, but the boy quickly regained his nerve.

"Well, tell me, how does it carry then; stand the jolt? And how are you going to unload it? Looks to me as if you're kidding. But I don't see any joke in it."

"Kidding? Indeed I'm not, man! But I can't stop now—"

"Oh, yes you will, too! My business is more important right now than yours. I want to see inside and I'm going to. You come here and open these doors for me!"

"What? Trying to act smart, ain't you?"
The little man was about to turn back to
his work, but Don caught him by the shoulder,
whirled him around and he gazed into the
muzzle of the boy's revolver.

"S-s-say, what you—?"

"Open those doors! There's a fellow in
there that's going back with us. He's in
there and I want him! Come on, open
that door and be quick about it. Wash,
bore a hole in this fellow if he makes a break!"

"S-say, put down that pistol! I haven't
done anything to you. Listen to reason:
there ain't anyone in there. The man who
was here—some fellow I don't know went
up the road. Guess he's a Frenchman."

"I guess he is—*not!*" said Don. "I know
him; saw him before in the United States
and up here near Montdidier. Come, open
up or chase him out!"

"I tell you there's explosives—"

"Bosh! Think I'm green; don't you?
Before I have to tell you again to open
those doors I'm going to blow the lock off
'em. Now, get busy!"

The weazen little man was most deliberate.
Coming around to the rear end of the ambulance, he reached up to the door latch. But

Don Caught Him by the Shoulder and Whirled Him
Around.

this action was a bluff—the boy felt sure of
that. The lad didn't feel like carrying out
his threat. To shoot through the doors
might kill someone and he didn't want to
kill. At most it was desirable to inflict
only a wound. Surely there must be a way
to win out here and Don had already learned
to depend on the power of his shooting-iron.
He had every inch of his nerve with him
at this moment.

"Can't open it, eh? Can't? Well, I'll
show you how then." He walked quickly
to the car and taking the revolver by the
chamber in his left hand—not a thing a
wise gunman would do at any time, under
stress of threatening circumstances he
caught the lower corner of one door that was
warped enough to gap at the bottom, and,
with a wrench he tore off the frail fastening.
The doors flew open.

The next instant Don was tumbling on
the ground, struggling to rise. He felt a
determination to fight, and hold this man
still uppermost in his mind, in spite of a
heavy blow over the head from within the
car. Where was his weapon? Why could
he not instantly regain his feet? Was that
the noise of the crippled car getting away?
Where was Wash? Why did he not shoot?

Then there was a period of unconsciousness until, a few minutes later, he did get to his feet to stare into the frightened eyes of Washington White.

"Oh, by cracky, they hit me and—they're gone! Wash, Wash, why didn't you shoot 'em? Why didn't you—?"

"Shoot nuthin'! Man, man, how come yo' lef' de barrel plum empty? Dey wuz no ca'tridge in de barrel. Ah cocked her 'en pulled de trigger 'en cocked her again 'en pulled 'en she wouldn't go off nohow 'en by de time Ah projecated whar de troble was, dem fellahs wuz a flyin' down de road lak Ol' Man Scratch wuz a huntin' 'em. But 'tain't so much Ah keer ef dey is gone so's yu ain' daid."

"Well, I care!" Don was clearly regaining his senses. "But it was my fault, Wash. I never thought to pump a cartridge into the barrel, and what a fool I was to pull that door open and not be ready. That villain was laying for me and, say, their car wasn't crippled much, either."

In the roadway, where the disabled car had stood, lay two monkey-wrenches and a small bolt which probably had pivoted a brake rod. At the rate of speed that car had started to gain, there would probably be no use for brakes!

"We've got to get back and report this fellow," Don said, returning his rifle to its case, and the revolver to its holster on his belt. "We've got only about twenty minutes' run yet, I think. Say, I feel like ten fools to let those devils get away. Keep your eye open for an M. P. on the road."

But not more than five minutes elapsed before the boys sighted a big touring car, with half a dozen khaki-clad men in it, tearing along toward them. Don stopped and signaled to the soldiers to do the same. They dashed up with screeching brakes, and Don stared. In the front seat, with the driver sat Clem Stapley.

All ill feeling in Don's mind was swept aside by the business at hand. Its nature and the comradeship that natives of the same distant country in a foreign land and in a common cause naturally abolish personal ill feeling. So he shouted:

"Hello, Clem! Say, fellows, there are two spies right ahead; they just—"

"In a Red Cross car?" asked a man on the rear seat; he was an M. P. "We're looking for them. Got word at the French evacuation hospital. Two did you say?"

"Yes, and they're getting away at a lively rate. Clem, one of them is the same German we saw in the train; the one that got away after they blew up the mills, over home. I've seen him before, too, north of here. He—"

"Sure he's a German?" asked the M. P. Clem had said no word and seemed to wish to avoid acknowledging Don. The M. P. turned to Clem.

"Say, Corp, if you know this spy we'd better be getting on. That's the orders. The P. C. told you to get these fellows."

Corporal Stapley turned slowly to reply. "Ask you informant here how he came to discover these Germans."

"Ask him yourself," retorted the M. P.

"Look here, Clem, don't be a fool—twice!" Don blurted, angrily. "This is big business and allows for no petty child's play."

"How did you get on to them?" Clem deigned to ask, then. And Don briefly related the adventure with the two signalers back of the Mondidier front and then told of the incident just past.

"Couldn't hold them," remarked Clem. "Fool trick. I guess you're better when you've got another that's some account backing you. Let them get away! Fierce! Poor work!"

"Hey, yo' white fellah, hit ain't so!" Wash put in, angrily. "Yu ain't in yo' right min', Ah reckon. Wha'd yu done ef yu'd ben thar?"

Clem paid no attention, but asked another question. "Did they scare you very much?"

Don, though hurt at his townsman's words, decided to let them pass; he merely waved his hand up the road, but Wash was more than game.

"Mah boss ain't gittin' scairt at nuthin', yo' white fellah! Ah bet yu can't scare him. Dis yer same German spy fit wif mah boss up yon furder no'th an' mah boss jes' up en' kilt dis German man's pardner, kilt him daid! Major Little of the evac. horspittle he done tol' me 'bout hit. Dey ain't no po' white German what kin scare mah boss!"

"Thank you, Wash. But this gentleman won't believe—"

"Well, you sassy nigger, how then did this spy get away?"

"Come, come, Corporal! This looks silly to me. Let us be going on, or that spy will get away from us."

"Good luck to you, Mister Policeman," said Don, and started his car again.

Don and Wash put in the rest of the day
everhauling the ambulance. Early in the
evening they were again on the road to
Château-Thierry and witnessing a sight most
depressing.

The French were in retreat—constantly
falling back. The retirement was orderly.
There was no rout, no apparent hurrying
and, from the din of battle ahead, it was
plain that every foot of advance that the
enemy made was bitterly contested. Yet
the Huns were gaining, as they had been
for five days and for nearly thirty miles,
encompassing an area of six hundred square
miles in this drive. Success seemed to be
written on their banners in this, the greatest
effort of all. Thus they forced a deep wedge
into the Allied line, the farthermost point
of which had reached the town of Château-
Thierry. And in the succeeding days what
more would they gain?

Back, and farther back were swept the
French, and the Huns were elated. The
blue-and-red clad troops who had fought
them so savagely were now no match for
the vast numbers of chosen shock troops.
Was there no means by which the boches
could be checked?

"By cracky, Wash, it looks as if these French had pretty nearly enough of it! I don't believe they have, though. But if they keep on coming this way we'll have to look sharp, or we'll run into a lot of Huns."

"Ah doan, want tuh run into no sich!" declared Wash. "Dey eats sauerkraut an' dis yere what dey calls limberburg cheese —an' oxcuse *me!*"

Beyond LaFerté the boys met platoons, companies, regiments, even battalions, or at least remnants of them, and all along the line more than a mile each side of Château-Thierry the falling back was certain and reg-gular.

Then, suddenly, almost as though dropped from the sky, came the Americans. From long distances in the rear and without stop-ping to rest from their arduous journey, the Yanks eagerly faced the Huns, and foremost among these cheerful, singing, jest-ing troops from overseas were the marines, leaving their train of parked lorries not far from LaFerté and coming up on foot.

The German High Command had received intelligence of the French handing the defense of this line nearest Paris over to the Yanks, and the word had come to the invaders:

"Go through these untrained Americans like a knife through cheese!" It is said that this was General Ludendorff's pet phrase.

The Americans took up their positions along the southern bank of the Marne and beyond in the hills. Then night came on. The enemy was too confident of a sweeping victory on the morrow to give serious thought to night attacks. Beyond a few minor skirmishes and some artillery firing, the hours of darkness passed uneventfully.

That night Don and Wash slept in their car, not far from the Château-Thierry road and within a short distance of some American regulars placed in reserve. Seeing the boys' fire, a few officers came over to talk. They were much interested in Don, and amused at Wash and his lingo. They also were free with certain information and opinions. One first-lieutenant who had most to say remarked:

"Well, we've got a job on our hands tomorrow, but we'll do it! These Frenchies are good fellows and good scrappers, but they have to follow fixed methods of fighting. This is not the American way. I say hang this trench business, pot shots, grenades, flares, sniping and all that!"

"Like to have a little of it kind of Indian fashion, eh?" suggested Don.

"That's it, my boy! Go right after them— rifle, bayonet and pistol!"

"I hear our commander told the general- issimo that we wanted to fight this in our own way," offered a young second-lieutenant.

"That's right. As soon as Foch said we might try, Pershing told him we could stop the Heinies, but we didn't want to follow the methods commonly in use. We wanted to go at them American fashion. So, those are the orders. And, believe me, we'll stop them all right!"

"Pretty sure of it?" queried Don.

"Certain, my boy; certain! How do you feel about it, Rastus!"

"Ah feels dis a-way 'bout hit:" answered Wash. "Whichaway a white man wants tuh fight Ah sez let him fight an' same way wif a niggah. Some goes at it wif fis' en' some wif a razzor, but fo' me lemme butt wif mah haid. Ah kin put mah weight back o' dis ol' bean o' mine en' make a dant in a grin' stone wif it!"

"Say, Rastus, go butt a Hun!"

"Show me one, boss; show me one! Ah ain't seed one yit what wants tuh fight. Ah on'y heerd tell of 'em."

CHAPTER XVI

Yanks

ASK Corporal Stapley to report here, Sergeant." A bluff Irishman, late of the regular army and now attached to the marines for his experience, saluted his Captain and turned to obey. A few minutes later he returned with the non-com.

"What luck, Stapley?" asked the Captain.

"Couldn't find them, sir," was the reply.

"That's bad. Made every effort, I suppose."

"We did, indeed. Jennings, of the Police, was with us and we scoured around thoroughly. A Red Cross ambulance is pretty easy to spot and we landed half a dozen, but they were all O. K."

"Haven't the least idea where those fellows could have gone?"

"Not the least. Case of mysterious disappearance. We thought they might have gone back to the base and we telephoned there to be on the lookout for them, and you may wager they are. We called from LaFerté

again later, but they hadn't seen them.
Jennings 'phoned both the Meaux and Paris
police to be on the watch."

"Unfortunate. Well, you did all you could.
Say, a little more personally: I see, by
the records, that you are a Brighton Academy
boy; is that right?"

"I am; class of 1919, but I don't know
what year we'll get through now."

"Well, let us hope it is not deferred.
Then college, eh?"

"I guess so."

"Brighton is a fine school. It was my
prep. school, too. I liked it immensely.
Good teachers, good courses, fine halls, splendid library, superb athletic field."

"I'm awfully glad to know you went there,
Captain. A good many of our fellows are
over here, or were in the service somewhere.
There's Herb Whitcomb—he's up in Flanders,
or was—and Roy Flynn, invalided home,
I believe. Some of the fellows are with the
flying force—two of my class, Jimmy Hill
and Dick Mann. Three of the older fellows,
two classes ahead of me, went into the navy.
Ted Wainwright and Jack Harris did, too,
and are on a submarine. Old Brighton did
its share!"

"Yes, and I heard of another from the school; he's a Red Cross ambulance driver; forget his name now. Only a youngster, but doing some great work. A yarn went around our camp about his landing on a couple of German spies and killing one of them. They said the boy had his own sporting rifle. Must be some plucky kid! Know him?"

"Perhaps I do," evaded Clem.

"Well, what I wanted to say is this: We go into action in the morning. The advance will be in formation by platoons. The units will keep together at first, but what will happen later, how much we shall become separated, no one can tell. I am going to keep an eye on you. If anything happens I'll do all in my power And I'm going to ask you, as an old Brighton boy, to do the same for me. Somehow, you know I feel as though it might be—that is, you see, there will be hard fighting and a great number of casualties and we must all do our best. We've got to make good and we shall. But some of us—I'm afraid a good many of us—won't come out of it—won't live to see the result. Here's my card, Stapley—my home address. My wife would like to know if—you understand."

"Yes, I understand, Captain. You may trust me."

"Thank you, Stapley. Hope you get along well at old Brighton when you get back. Good luck! Taps will sound in about half an hour. Sorry you didn't find those spies They may turn up yet."

The young corporal left the spot and went to where his own platoon was bivouacked. The men, officers and all, slept scattered on the ground, to avoid casualties from stray shells. Each man had a blanket and poncho and though the temperature was low for June, the nights being chilly, it was ideal camping weather for men long hardened to it. Some of the toughest fellows had no more than thrown a corner of the blanket across their shoulders, sleeping in their clothes and removing only their shoes. It was the order to do this, as marching feet need an airing and, better, a dabble in cool water. A little stream ran near by and one might safely wager, where it emptied into the Marne, the water that night ran black with the soil of France.

Morning dawned clear and breezy. Shortly after reveille, a messenger arrived from the American headquarters and another from

the French Field Staff. Half an hour later
the two regiments of marines, moving like
one man, were marching straight across
country a little to the northwest of Château-
Thierry. It was the intention to drive the
Huns out of their threatening positions in
the hills where they were concentrating troops
and artillery, mostly machine-gun units. A
brigade also of the Third Division U. S.
Regulars, moved forward at nearly the same
time in support of the marines, if needed.

No prettier sight could be imagined than
those long lines of soldiers, over two thousand
in number, sweeping forward. They had been
called "the Matchless Marines" and by
another equally expressive, though homlier
name, "the Leathernecks." Picked men,
every one of them chosen with regard to
his athletic and probable fighting ability,
they could but live up to the standards set
for them by their predecessors in the same
force, adhering always to the maxims that
"the marines never retreat" and that "they
hold what they've got."

The peeping sun shone upon their brown
uniforms and glistened on their bayoneted
guns, as they moved through waving grass
and over fields of yellowing grain. There

was no sound of drum or fife. No band
played martial music—that is not the custom
when a modern army goes against the enemy—
but here and there along those steady,
triple lines could be heard laughter, snatches
of song, the voice of some wag bantering
his fellows.

The orders to the commanding general
of the division ran something like this:
Rout the enemy from the village of Bouresches. Break up the machine-gun and artillery positions in Belleau Woods and if possible capture Hill No. 165. Consolidate
positions at these points and south of the
village of Torcy and hold them.

It was evident that the commander-in-
chief depended fully on "the Leathernecks"
and felt confident that they would do as
ordered, although they had before them
a large undertaking. It was known that the
Germans had two divisions of picked troops
at this point, with still another division in
reserve.

There was double reason for this confidence.
The Americans had already been performing
most creditably within the sector about
Château-Thierry. A few days before a strong
detachment of American regular troops had

withstood an attack of the enemy at Veuilly
Wood, nine miles north of the Marne, and
had driven them back. The day following
a detachment of machine gunners had held
the approaches to the bridges across the
Marne, connecting the north and the south
towns of Château-Thierry itself and prevented
the Huns from crossing, while a battalion
of Americans, supporting French artillery
that was pounding the Huns in the northern
end of the town, captured and wiped out
more than their number of Germans who had
managed to gain the south bank by pontoons.
On the same day the Third and Twenty-
eighth Divisions of U. S. regulars, commanded
by a French officer, had defeated the enemy
in his attempt to make a crossing of the
Marne at Jaulgonne, a few miles east of
Château-Thierry, and had driven him back
to his former positions. But all these battles,
relatively small actions in themselves, had
been fought according to European methods,
and had been directed by French generals
and aided by French infantry and artillery.

The action now about to take place was
to be that of the Americans alone, under
American staff direction, and the boys were
going into it tickled with the idea of being

allowed in their own way to get a whack at the Huns.

Corporal Stapley, as he trudged along with his squad, thought of a good many things of a rather solemn nature, though not once did he permit a hint of this to bother his fellows. The next in line was a wag named Giddings, but Clem noted that the youth was very quiet now, and that his face was pale. With a laugh Clem turned to the fellow: "Say, Gid, it's a fine day for this little picnic."

"Wonder when the strawberries and ice cream will be served," Giddings remarked and Clem knew that no matter how the young man really felt he was game. The corporal glanced down the line; there were other pale faces and set lips, but there were also smiles and laughter. One man struck up a song, with words and music *ad libitum:*

> "Where do we go from here, boys,
> Where do we go from here?
> To punch the Hun
> Like a son-of-a-gun.
> It'll be some fun
> To make him run
> And get his bun
> And take his mon.
> Oh, hi, yi, that's where we'll go from here!"

Some joined in. Laughter broke out down
the line. One chap began to whistle the
Sailor's Hornpipe and another, in a deep
bass voice, tried to put impromptu words
to it, after the manner of the popular version
concerning "de debbil," but without much
poetic success:

> "Did you ever see the Heinie
> With his skin all black and spiny
> A–diggin' in the trenches
> With his big toe nail?"

And another laugh followed, but it was cut
short by a shell which tore through the air
only a little above the heads of the men,
and exploded not a hundred feet behind the
last line. It was immediately followed by
a second that landed about the same distance
from the front of the first line and ricocheted,
turning and twisting, then lying still—not
ten steps ahead of the line. There was a
little squirming, and two fellows were obliged
to step almost over the menacing thing.
Pulling down their steel helmets and lowering
their heads, they veered apart, while some
arms went up in front of faces and eyes.
But the shell proved a "dud." Had it exploded it would doubtless have sent half a dozen
boys to the graveyard and the hospital.

"One back and one front and the next one—"

"A clean miss!" shouted Clem.

The words were no more than said when his prediction came true. The shell went high and wide. But that which immediately followed was of a far more deadly character than shells. Shrapnel and whiz-bangs could not cover the ground, but it seemed as though the rain of machine-gun bullets that suddenly swept down from the thickets and rocks of the great hillside which loomed ahead must reach every inch of space.

"Double quick! Charge!" came the order, echoed from mouth to mouth by under-officers and still, like one man, that khaki-clad host went at it on the run. Every man saw that the more quickly the work was done the better chances he and his fellows had for surviving that leaden hail.

"Smash 'em! Tear 'em to pieces!" Clem found himself yelling again and again and he heard similar shouts on all sides of him.

"Give 'em ballyhoo!" howled young Giddings.

And they did—if that expresses something like annihilation! Before the Huns could do more than fire a round or two from a score of well-placed machine-guns on the hillside the marines, like waves of avenging devils, were upon them with a fury that those long-practised death-dealers of the Fatherland had not before experienced and totally unprepared for. They were used to seeing their accurate shooting from such an array of fire-spitters stop their enemies and drive them back but no such result was in evidence now.

Many of the Huns broke and ran, some tried to hide, some threw up their hands and shouted: "Kamerad! Kamerad!" A few stuck to their guns until overpowered, and died fighting. Many, threatened with the bayonet, surrendered at once. And the marines went yelling on, overtaking the fleeing Germans, stabbing to death, shooting or clubbing with rifles those who still resisted. Breaking up the machine-gun nests, they rounded up the prisoners until the hillside was entirely in American hands. Then the Yanks halted and sought shelter from the German artillery which now began to throw shells upon the eastern and northern side of the hill from enemy positions beyond. On the southwestern slope, where they were out of danger from this fire, the victorious regiments re-formed for further duty, bringing in all scattered units and trying to count the cost.

The taking of the hill had not been entirely one-sided, except in the matter of a victory. The machine-gunners had been placed in position to hold this strategic bit of ground and to make it hot for those who attempted to take it from them, and they were past masters at that sort of thing. The reception they gave the marines exacted a heavy toll.

Following fast upon the heels of the men from overseas came the wonderfully efficient American Red Cross. Ambulances rushed across the fields, many of carrying capacity only, a few fitted up for field dressing stations. Doctors and nurses, braving the enemy shells, attended the most urgent cases only, sending the majority back to the newly established evacuation hospitals which had, within two days, supplanted those of the overtaxed French, or to the bases that also had moved nearer this fighting front.

And so everywhere on the hillside up which the marines had so gloriously charged, the *brancardiers* moved with their stretchers, rapidly bringing away the wounded, whether friend or foe. And the officers who were still on duty went about among the men, detailing squads here and there for burial duty and to help and comfort their unfortunate companions. It was the work of a little more than two hours.

CHAPTER XVII

Victory

CLEM STAPLEY stood leaning on his rifle gazing far away over the green fields and woodlands of that beautiful, rolling country, not unlike his own homeland. The boy's thoughts were filled with memories; the reaction from the strenuous experiences of the minutes just past caused him to sway a little on his feet. His company's second-lieutenant, passing near, turned and looked into the boy's pale face.

"Hurt eh? Can you walk? Better get back—"

"No, sir. No! Only a trifle. A scratch on the arm; spent bullet went up my sleeve like one of those black ants. I shook it out."

"Let me see," ordered the officer. Clem bared his arm and showed a long white and blue welt from wrist to elbow. On the fleshy part the skin had broken, and blood was trickling down.

"Go get it bandaged."

"I can do it, if someone—"

"Help him, Terry. Get his jacket and shirt off. Use a little iodine. You'll be all right."

"Are we going on, sir, soon?" Clem asked.

"Very soon. To the village over the next rise, about three miles from here. Bouresches they call it."

"I want to find my squad and tell them about poor Giddings. Have you seen my Captain?"

"Dead. At the bottom of the hill. Lieutenant Wells, too. I am in command now. Was Giddings—?"

"Yes. Went down while he was getting off a joke about a Hun who was yelling for mercy. When we turned to let some others of a gun crew have it—they had their gun trained on us—a brute fired at Giddings at about five steps. But I got the skunk with the bayonet and then Davidson and I went on and got two of the other gun-crew. The others of both crews surrendered; Jones' squad, coming up, took them in. Then I got hit."

A bugle call echoed sweetly along the slope. A sergeant came running up the hill, calling right and left to officers. He passed the lieutenant and Clem.

"Orders from the General. Form quick in place in the road due south of the hill. Headquarters down there now. Enemy attack from the east. We are to hold support positions."

Again and again the bugle call sounded from the road. There was some lively running about and falling in. Then once more, in broken formations, the marines descended and under rapid orders lined up, partly along this old road, behind a low bank, and somewhat sheltered by a row of trees. Some of the regulars came up and formed beyond, in the same line. The rest were held in reserve farther back. At the left some regiments of French infantry stretched the line, making a front of about two miles. Fully half a mile to the east a French division occupied the first line facing the enemy positions.

Corporal Clem's arm hurt considerably. A member of his squad had treated and bandaged it with materials out of a first aid kit. But the wound was becoming more and more painful, and his arm began to stiffen. He could not understand why he should feel sick at the stomach and hungry at the same time. The "Leathernecks" had not

12

eaten since breakfast, and it was now well on in the afternoon.

Clem looked about him, for misery loves company. There were wide gaps in the line, though that was anything but comforting. It was horribly depressing to think that some of these cronies, jolly good fellows all, would now be dumped under the sod, and that others were never more to walk, nor to know the joy of health. Perhaps some would never see nor hear again. Many less seriously injured would bear scars all their lives.

Martin there, formerly next in line to Giddings, and now next to Clem, had his head elaborately done up in two-inch bandages. Replying to a question he said, jovially:

"When I get back to God's country, I am going to take this old pan of a hat, hang it up in the prettiest place in the best room in the house and keep it covered with fresh flowers. Why? The darned old thing saved my life. I wouldn't 'a' had any bean left if this inverted wash basin thing hadn't been covering it."

"Poor Giddings always had a pick at his helmet," remarked Clem. "He used to say that just a hat wasn't much good and that what a man wants in this war is a suit of armor made out of stove plates. In his case he was about right."

"But wrong in mine," said Martin.

"Say, what's doing, Sarge?" asked a private of the non-com in the next squad, who now stood next to Clem in the line-up.

"The Heinies are going to make a push here, I believe," was the answer.

"When?"

"Pretty soon. Guess we'll hear the barrage laid down first. But maybe they think they're strong enough to rush us without that."

"Hope they do. It's more lively. I don't like them barrages. Make me think o' my old uncle across the pond. He's one o' those bear hunters. Sez he'd a heap rather fight a bear than a hive o' bees; you can see the bear."

"Right-o! Here, too! You can stick a bayonet into a Hun, but you can't even dodge these here mowin'-machine bullets."

"Listen, fellows!" Clem held up his hand.

A distant shot, another, several, a dozen, a thousand, crack, bang, boom, as though all the Fourth of July celebrations that ever had been and ever would be had been turned loose at once.

"She's on, boys! And there'll be a lot of ricocheting bullets coming this far—so look out for them!" So spoke the lieutenant, now commander of Clem's company, as he walked up and down the line.

The sergeant next to Clem turned to the officer.

"Do you think the Frogeaters can hold them, lieutenant?"

"Doubt it. They say the Huns outnumber them three to one. And they mean to drive right through to the Compiègne road. So it's up to us to stop them, I guess."

"We'll try hard, lieutenant," Clem offered.

Within twenty minutes the roar of the barrage ceased as suddenly as it began. Then came a lull, followed by the rattle of small arms which, at the distance, sounded much like a lot of youngsters cracking hickory nuts. Within half an hour after this the expected happened. For the tired and greatly outnumbered French, fighting savagely, had failed to stem the Hun tide and began to give way before it. Some retreated a little too late and these were quickly surrounded and taken prisoner, to suffer tortures in German detention camps for many a long day. The wounded were hurried to the rear.

As the dressing stations to the extreme right of the support line became congested those set up in sheltered positions directly behind the hill were called on for duty. Then the many ambulances of the United States army, French army and American Red Cross dashed through the line of marines, and around the base of the hill.

It was at once a solemn and a cheering sight. However horrible this war of science and ingenuity had become, it reacted in greater humanity than has ever been known.

The sound of an automobile horn in front caused Clem to look up and he was almost face to face with Don Richards. The younger lad was about to look away, but he quickly chose to salute his townsman. The corporal nodded stiffly as Don passed on.

The sound of rifle fire interspersed with the cloth-ripping noise of machine-guns and the detonation of heavier artillery, began to come nearer. A company of French infantry, marching in perfect order, but in quick time, appeared in the distance. It wheeled sharply and passed to the south, around the extreme right of the Americans. In a few minutes it was followed by other and larger contingents, a regiment in part,

with great gaps in its ranks, a battalion of
machine gunners, each squad with its wicked
mitrailleuse, ammunition handcarts, more
infantry and still more until very soon they
had thinned out to scattered and broken
units, often without officers. Many of these
came up and passed through the American
lines.

The expressions on the faces of these French
soldiers told of varied emotions. Some were
morose, angry, or despairing. Others laughed
and jested. Some smiled and wore an air
of undying confidence. Clem had learned
too little French so far to understand their
rapid utterances, but the lieutenant stood
near him, talking with a French subaltern
who spoke excellent English and who began
to question the retreating soldiers. There
was a nasal babble and then the translation,
with some remarks, to the lieutenant. Clem
easily caught much of it.

"He says the enemy was too strong for
them; that there must be half a million
men. But I think that an exaggeration."

"This fellow says that the enemy came
at them, swarming like ants. It is no use,
he says, to try to check them now; they
are irresistible."

"This man declares that they are many, but they are not overwhelming, and that if the retreat had not been ordered we could have held the enemy awhile."

"He says that it is no use to try to stop them—they come like a tidal wave."

"This fellow hopes you Americans may stop them."

"He says if there had only been a few more of us we could have stopped them."

"Here is one who insists that Paris is doomed, and all is lost. But, you see, his companion was killed by his side."

The officers moved rapidly away and then, almost suddenly, there was an end of the retreating French. The ambulances also had ceased in their errands of mercy over the ground ahead. A strange hush fell upon everything but the forces of nature. The breeze toyed with the wheat. Birds sang blithely; across the fields a cow was lowing, a poor creature, perhaps that a farmer who had suddenly vacated his home before the oncoming Huns, had failed to drive along toward the west.

The lieutenant passed along the line again, speaking to his men. He was a young man, tall, with fine square shoulders, a firm jaw and a pleasant voice—every inch a soldier. He paused a moment and said to Clem:

"Your arm is better now? Well, try to think it is. You'll need it. I hope it won't interfere with your sleep tonight." Then to the sergeant, in answer to a question: "Yes, they're coming; re-forming first. There are enough of them to make us sit up and take notice. Three divisions to our one and a half. I don't think any of us will take a nap during the next hour or so. But, remember, we've got to give them all there is in us! Keep cautioning your men to shoot low, to keep their heads, see their hind-sights, and try to hit what they aim at. It will be just like target practice, boys; only more so. Every time you score means that's one less chance of your being scored on."

Anticipation often goes reality "one better," to use a betting phrase. The waiting for the expected battle was most irksome—nerve-racking to some. It cannot be a joyful thing to contemplate the killing of human beings, even though they are bent on killing. Upon such occasions minutes drag by like hours. It is an actual relief when the end of the suspense is at hand.

Clem glanced at his wrist watch—it was

4:45. The enemy could be seen now in the
distance, advancing steadily. They were
coming on in mass formation straight across
the waving wheat that the retreating French
had avoided trampling down. The Huns
gloried in this destruction. They were going
to make this place a shambles with dying
and dead when they should occupy this
region. They would turn it into a desert of
burned homes, felled trees, girdled orchards,
ruined villages and looted factories—as all
the territory they had thus far occupied had
been desolated.

"Cut loose, boys! The range is nearly
flat. Don't fire too high. Now, then, every
man for himself!" Thus ran the orders
along the line and the crack of the rifles
this time meant more to the advancing
Germans than ever before. The French
subaltern, sent to observe the behavior of
the Americans went into ecstasies after the
manner of his race. With eyes sticking
out so far that there was danger of his butting
into something and knocking them off, he
watched the "Leathernecks" in long-range
rifle action awhile; then he hurried back
to his staff. Shortly he was back again with
some higher officers of the French supporting

line, and their enthusiasm was unbounded.
The subaltern translated liberally:

"*Voila!* Your men shoot! *Sacre!* They are
deliberate! They see their sights! They
hit the mark! The Huns stop—they waver!
Ah, they come on again! True they are
brave men! And they obey their officers—also
brave men! But behold again! The front
rank is down, gone! What say you? Yes,
wiped out! And still they come again?
Ah now, it is too much. They lose all if
they remain. Behold, they break! They
retreat! They hide in the wheat! They
creep away!"

"Cut that wheat all to pieces, boys!
Don't let any of them get away!" ordered
the lieutenant, repeating a common order
and it was just what the marines were doing.

Clem, with a hot gun, turned a moment
to speak to the officer. "Are our machine-
gun crews at work?" he asked.

"Yes, over there by that clump of trees.
I never saw those lads do better work. I
think those Huns have about enough. We
win!"

"Any of our boys hurt?" asked the sergeant.

"A machine-gun crew of the enemy con-
centrated on one part of our right and did

some damage," said the officer. "Two of their shrapnel burst among the doughboys to the south, I hear. Otherwise, I believe—"

"Nobody got hit here," asserted the sergeant.

"They didn't think it worth while to lay down a second barrage and their infantry hardly fired a shot," laughed the officer.

"Got badly fooled," said the sergeant. "Why don't we go after them now?"

"I suppose our commander thinks they're whipped enough and there are Hun batteries to the east of the hill that must be dislodged first. Hello, another air scrap is going to be pulled off!"

Five German planes were coming along, pretty low and in line, their evident intention being to seek revenge by bombing the line of "Leathernecks." But four French battle-planes swept over to meet them, one fellow swooping low to cheer the marines for their splendid work. Two German fighting machines were high overhead in support of the big bombing planes.

The French and American light field-pieces got busy and made it so hot for the foremost plane that it turned and retreated, trying to come back higher up. But by that time the French planes had driven the others back, sending one down in flames behind the German lines. The guns turned their attention to smashing a German battery going into position beyond the wheat field and performed this duty admirably, dismounting all of the three German guns and killing every man with them. The Hun battle-planes, refusing to fight and retreating, had given two of the French planes a chance to signal the range to Allied batteries.

The day was fast coming to a close. When the marines and their supporters had broken ranks and bivouacked for the night Corporal Stapley went to the commanding officer of his company and asked if he might go over to the hill and visit the captain's grave.

"He was an old Brighton boy and that is my school," Clem said, "and he asked me if I would tell his wife, if anything happened to him. I thought I should like to write her—all that she would care to know."

"Go ahead, Stapley; that's a noble purpose. I'll give you a note to enclose, saying how much we appreciated him and how bravely he met his fate. Take one of the men with you—some fellow that specially liked the captain. Get back at dark."

CHAPTER XVIII

Bushwhacking

IT was half a mile back to the southern side of the hill where the bloody engagement of the morning had taken place and a like distance to the little plot of ground in the corner of a field where some of the American dead were buried. Clem and Private Martin easily found the captain's resting-place.

Some sappers were still at work, and a slightly wounded staff-officer of the marines had been detailed to keep record of the burials. One fellow, his identification number and all papers about his person missing, had not been recognized nor interred. On the way back Clem glanced down at this unfortunate.

"It's poor Giddings!" he exclaimed.

"What? Not that joker in your company?" protested the officer.

Clem nodded; Martin confirmed this. The lads helped to lower their comrade into his grave and stood with bowed heads during the brief reading of the burial service. Then they went into the field near by and made two wreaths of poppies and daisies to hang on the wooden crosses over Giddings and the captain.

The shadows were growing long; the two "Leathernecks" had quite a distance to travel in the return to camp. For a little way their road lay along the foot of the hill around which a well beaten track had been made by motor cars and artillery. Now and then they were met by ambulances plying between the dressing station west of the hill and of the last battle-field where the marines and regulars had repulsed the German advance. Some of the cars detoured part way up the hillside by a farm lane, on the slopes to seek further for wounded that might have been overlooked.

The driver of a passing ambulance, returning from the dressing station, offered to give the boys a lift and they accepted gladly. They ran on for less than a fourth of a mile when something got out of order with a spark plug which they stopped to replace, just beyond the lane turning up the hill.

"Be only a moment," the driver said. "I'll get you fellows right by your camp in ten minutes."

"Plenty of time!" both said and, while Martin aided the driver a little, Clem walked to an opening in the thicket and gazed up to where, in the morning, he had seen such bloody work with rifle, pistol and bayonet.

Another ambulance came along the road. It seemed to Clem that he had heard the motor start somewhere back under the hill, though there could be nothing strange in that. There was an unusually large Red Cross in its patch of white on the side of the long, low car, and the machine glided along as though it possessed great motive force but was held down in speed. Two men were in the seat. When the car reached the lane it swung in and, without apparent slowing, ascended the grade, stopping about half way up. A few yards beyond it was an army ambulance, its driver walking away across the slope.

Clem's very brief glance at the driver of the Red Cross car had caused him to start and wonder. He hardly knew why he gazed after the car with an unpleasant feeling, and then, in order to watch its movements, crossed the road and swung himself up on a branch of a low tree.

There were no other cars on the hill and

apparently no other people, but the army ambulance man. Clem was cogitating:

"Now, can't I think where? What had Don Richards said only yesterday? Spies? But would they dare again to come here boldly and—" his thoughts were cut short.

A man got down from the long, low car and quickly went to the other machine. He paused and looked about for a moment, then raised the hood and seemed to be working rapidly. He put down the hood and returned. Then the Red Cross car moved on rapidly up the hill to the far end of the lane, where it turned across pasture ground and veered about among the rocks and thickets, stopping presently on the southeast slope.

"Fire and flinders! It is—it is!" exclaimed Clem. "They wouldn't dare to go so far east and expose themselves to the guns unless the Huns knew and approved of it."

The boy dropped to the ground and, taking pad and pencil from his pocket, wrote the following:

"I beg leave to report that I have this moment discovered the Hun spies we were after yesterday. They have gone to the eastern side of Hill 165, probably to signal the German lines, as reported before. I also saw them disable an army ambulance. Fearing to fail in their arrest, and confident that I can accomplish this with the aid of the ambulance man on the hill, I take the liberty of delaying my return to post. Will report as soon as possible.

CLEMENT STAPLEY, Corporal.

This sheet he folded, addressed, and handed to his companion, Martin. The ambulance had a new spark plug and was ready to start.

"Give this to the lieutenant as soon as you get in," Clem said. "Now, please don't ask any questions. I'm on an expedition the captain ordered yesterday and the lieutenant knows about it. You might tell him I said so. And, by the way, got any extra cartridges for your pistol? I might need them. I left mine in my kit. Will pay you back when I get back."

"Maybe I could help you," began Martin, but Clem backed off.

"No; I can handle this. Nothing much. When I come in I think you'll see me bringing some Heinies along—pretty soon, too."

Clem alone, hurried up the hill by the lane. He had but one purpose. His mind was singularly free from any thought of strategy as he went straight to the seat of the trouble. He meant simply to arrest these men and prove their guilt afterward. He reached the army ambulance and saw the driver returning with a wounded man's arm over his shoulder. This soldier could walk, but he had been shot through the shoulder and had lain unconscious for a time in a shell hole, where he was overlooked. Clem recognized him as a member of his own company. The man smiled and tried to salute.

"Driver, I'll help this man along. I think when you look at your engine you'll find something wrong with it. I saw it done— from the road down yonder."

The driver raised his engine hood. "Well, I should say! Look at that; will you? Every plug wire cut away and gone and the plugs smashed. Do you know who did this?"

"I think I can introduce you to the parties responsible. They're right up there on the hill now," Clem replied; then turned to the wounded soldier. "We want to get you in right away and—"

"You let me rest here a bit, Corp. I won't

be any worse off and you go and get those devils. I bet they're Heinies, drat 'em! I'd like to know some more of them are going the long road, even if I go the same."

"You're going to be all right, man."

"Not on your life, Corp. Never. A fellow always knows when he's got his for good and all!"

"Don't believe it," said Clem. We'll take you to the dressing station in that car of theirs shortly, unless another ambulance comes up here. Then you'd better go with it. Now, then, Mr. Driver, you look pretty husky. Feel like having a scrap?"

"I could cut the heart out of the weasel that disabled my car! That is if it was just 'rough-house.' I expect he's got a gun with him."

"Likely enough—haven't you?" asked Clem.

"Why yes—in the car—army pistol. But I guess I'm not much at using it. I'm better with a knife. It's either the gun or me, but I can't hit a barn door up against it. I can shoot with a real gun, though. I've hunted and shot deer."

"Well, then, bo, all you've got to do," suggested the wounded man, "is to chase back to that shell hole and get my rifle. She's there; I forgot to fetch her. And she's a dandy old pill-slinger, too, believe me."

Ten minutes later the two young fellows went up to the end of the lane and turned sharply to the right, as Clem had seen the suspected Red Cross car do. It was now growing dusk, though the boys could easily make their way across the field. Clem had noticed a bunch of trees taller than those around on the edge of the woods below the summit of the hill, and that the top of one of these trees was partly cut off and hanging, the work of a shell. It was beyond this spot that the spies' car had stopped.

"We're getting there," whispered the driver. "The Heinies are liable to send some whiz-bangs over here any time."

"I hardly think so while that fellow is here," Clem said. "We'll see if I'm not right pretty soon. We'll have to risk it, anyway."

"Go ahead; I've risked more than that more than once."

"What is your name?"

"Duncan. I'm from Maine. What's yours?"

"Stapley. Marines. I'm from Pennsylvania. Go easy now; we're getting up near the place and they'll likely be watching out for somebody. Let's wait until it's a little darker, then sneak up. I have a hunch those chaps are on this side signaling information to their friends over east."

The darkness grew thicker and gave way to night. The watchers had found shelter, both against possible German shells or discovery, behind a boulder where they crouched for several minutes. No shells came that way, though the booming of cannon not very far away to the east and northeast showed that the Huns were awake and replying to the constant cannonading of the French and Americans. All around the boys it was as quiet as any night in early summer. Once, overhead, they heard the call of a night bird and once the twitter of some small feathered citizen disturbed in its slumbers in a thicket. There was the squeak of a mouse or shrew beneath the turf almost at their feet. In a whisper that could not have been heard twenty feet away Clem told his companion what he suspected, from his recollection of the doubtful ambulance driver's face and from Don Richards' brief account of the signaling near Mont-

didier. After what Clem had seen here and
the injury to the army ambulance, there
was enough to satisfy Duncan that they
had Hun spies to deal with.

"I'm going to get up and take a look
round," he said. "Going to be an old dead
tree; it's a trick we Indians pull off to fool
moose. You see I've got a little Indian
blood in me. Fact. Proud of it." And with
that Duncan crawled up on the boulder and
slowly stood up, his arms extended crookedly,
one held higher than the other. Thus he
remained for several minutes. Then he came
down, even more slowly.

"Say, pard, you've got the dope. They're
up there all right, about two hundred yards,
and they're signaling. There's a light going
up and down. bull's eye, turned away,
but I could see the reflection on a rock."

"Well, we're here to stop that and get
those fellows," said Clem. "Shall we rush
them?"

"No, no! We'd only give them a fine
chance to bore us full of holes. They don't
want to be surprised, you can bet. But we
can stalk them, as we do bear on high ground,
and work the bird call so as to make them
think nobody's around in our direction.
Are you on?"

"I am! Say, I guess you are Indian all right. You lead off—and I'll follow and do just as you do, as near as I can."

"Only be careful where you put your hands and knees. Don't crack any sticks nor roll any stones. Ready?"

Clem wondered at first whether the method would prove successful. It loomed up like a large undertaking, considering the distance. Would it not be better to just march right up on the spies and trade gun-fire with them, if need be? But the farther the boys progressed the more Clem became convinced that this was the only means of surprising the enemy. The nature of the ground was such that any one walking boldly up could have been seen first by the spies, and held up or shot. Fortunate, indeed, was it that this fellow Duncan was on the hill. Truly a wonderful chap when it came to this sort of thing.

Slowly they went, on hands and knees, for another fifty feet or more, stopping every little while to listen, and Duncan made a soft twittering sound exactly like the little bird in the thicket below. Presently he rose cautiously to take a look and get the bearings, after which he turned and put his lips to Clem's ear.

"Man on watch about a hundred feet from us, sitting on a rock. He don't look this way. I think I'd better edge off a little and work around so as to come up on the other chap, and you work up nearer this one, behind the thicket. When I yell he'll turn and then you've got him. Wait till I yell."

There is little doubt that this plan would work out well. The German mind can not cope in matters of woodcraft and ambush with that of an American backwoodsman. Duncan wormed himself away and Clem could not detect a sound made in his progress. Hardly more than fifteen minutes would be required for him to gain his object, but in less than five minutes a whistle sounded up the hill. The watcher ran that way and there was the buzz of a self-starter and the whir of a motor. Before the bushwhackers had time to collect their senses the long car, with its lights on, was running back across the field.

Duncan joined Clem. "Rotten luck! But glad you didn't shoot. And say, they've got to go slow over and around those rocks. Can't we head 'em off if we go down the hill straight toward the foot of the lane? How're your legs?"

"I'm with you!" announced Clem, and together, with the easy, long-stepping lope of the runner trained in the woods, the two set off, leaping over the obstacles in their way, dodging around boulders and thicket patches, and making good time in spite of the uneven ground.

But they had not covered a third of the distance and had several hundred yards yet to go when they saw that the chase was hopeless. The car had made far better time than they had believed possible and when it reached the head of the lane it turned and shot like an arrow down the hill.

The boys stopped and gazed in bitter disappointment after the retreating foemen.

"I wish we had sailed into them up yonder," Clem said.

"Gettin' shot ourselves would have been worse than this," Duncan argued.

"Say, look, they've stopped! About where your car is!" Clem exclaimed. "Maybe we can—"

Duncan raised the army rifle as though to bring it into position for firing. "If it wasn't so blamed dark I could get 'em," he declared. "Anyway, I can make a try." But Clem stopped him.

"Hold on, man! You may hit the wounded man there!"

"Blazes! Never thought of it. Can't risk that. Couldn't stop 'em, anyhow; not in a million shots, with only their lights to shoot at."

"There they go on again. We're licked this time," Clem said, mournfully. "Come on; let's get back to the lane. I'll help you make that poor chap comfortable. Then I'll go down and try to get another ambulance. I've got to get back to camp pretty soon. Say, it's going to be tough to have to admit we couldn't arrest those spies. It's what I stayed out for and sent word to the lieutenant that I could do. He'll be sore, and Martin will rub it into me for a month. Say, those spies have put out their lights now."

Duncan mumbled something about their running on with lights out to avoid being recognized. He hoped they'd run into a shell hole and break their blamed necks. The young down-east woodsman was grievously put out not to avenge himself on the men who damaged his ambulance.

Not another word was exchanged between the two youths while they were crossing the open ground to the lane. They reached and turned down the well-worn road a little above the ambulance.

"He's asleep, I guess," Clem said, glancing at the soldier lying on the cot that Duncan had spread for him. The *ambulancier* went over and stooped down to look at or speak to the wounded man. Then he straightened up with a jerk and stepped back. Though his nerves were of steel after the many bitter experiences following battles, raids, artillery fire and gas attacks, he must have had a sharp prod at the sight that met him. It is one thing to see men killed, maimed, blown to pieces in fair fighting, but quite another thing to find one foully murdered outside of the area of fighting.

"Killed!—stabbed! They've killed him! Those—those devils!" His voice was thick with rage.

Clem could only weakly repeat part of this—it was too horrible for mere words. Instinctively they both turned to gaze down the lane again toward where the spies had fled. And suddenly, from the bottom of the hill, the two bright lights of an approaching ambulance glared at them ominously.

CHAPTER XIX

BOURESCHES

STAPLEY and Duncan with their weapons ready, waited, crouching. In their agitation they had not observed other ambulances coming along the road at the foot of the hill and they did not doubt that the spies, seeing no light and not suspecting the return of the *ambulancier* whose car they had broken and whose passenger they had killed, might be returning perhaps to lie in wait for him. They seemed to be having things all their own way of late so why should they not try to accomplish more?

The glaring lights came nearer. The throbbing motor had easily the better of hills such as this. The seekers of a just revenge tried to see who was on the driver's seat behind the lights—a difficult thing to do. A voice caused their weapons to lower.

"Reckon dis de place t' stop. One amberlance done quit gittin' all het up, heah. Yu kin turn her roun' easy by backin' into de fiel' a ways, lessen yu hits a groun'hawg hole er sumpin'."

"No groundhogs in this country, Wash. We might hit a rock, though. Hello, you fellows! Are you stuck?" This last addressed to Duncan and Stapley who had risen and come forward.

If Clem felt any bitterness toward Don he did not think of it now; there was too much else to occupy his mind. But Don, leaping to the ground instantly, seemed not to know him. Duncan knew Don and at once began to relate their experiences.

"And you mean to say you fellows couldn't stop them? Let them get away up yonder and murder this poor helpless soldier on the way! And only yesterday this fellow," with a bend of his head he referred to Clem, "rubbed it into me because—"

"Well, that—that was dif—" began Clem.

"Not a bit of it! But why parley? Duncan, you and I can get busy. Those fellows are down there yet, in the road just west of the lane. They're doing something to their car. That's twice I've run into them fixing it, but I didn't know them this time. Wash, confound you, were you asleep? Why didn't you tell me—?"

"Sleep yuse'f! How's I know—?"

"Cut the comedy! Come on, if you're sure that was the spies," Clem said.

"Hold on! You're not in this and they'll be there awhile, you can bet," said Don. "You fellows slipped up in your attempt and this is my job. There's one way to get those chaps and that only, Duncan. Listen to me—Wash, you get in back and lie low. We two will get in on the front seat. We'll dim the lights and then go along singing and let on we're half tipsy until we get right up to them. I'll stop and ask them for a drink and you turn the bull's-eye on them and if it's the spies we'll act quick; see?"

"I'm going with you," said Clem.

"Not in my car," Don retorted. But Clem walked to Don's ambulance and jumped in.

"We can scrap afterwards, Richards; not now. Come on—three are better than two."

"That's so," asserted Duncan.

The plan was carried out as laid down. With all their science and suspicions those Hun spies had no idea of any such thing being pulled off. Though three half-drunk Yankees were an unusual sight, especially in an ambulance, it was nothing to bother about. To humor them and let them go on was a simple matter.

"Oh, we won't go home till evenin'!" sang Clem.

"Till mornin', you blamed fool! D-don't ye know the words?" Don shouted, tickled to give Clem a dig. "Aw, dry up an' let me sing it! Thish-a-way it goes: Oh, we won't get home till mornin', till broad-s-say—."

With a grinding of brakes the ambulance came to a sudden stop, almost even with the long, low car by the roadside. "S-say," continued Don, "any—you blokes got a drink? One good service man to another; eh, friend? Just a little nip—you fellers are Red Cross, ain't you? Eh? Les' see—. Hands up! Both of you, quick! One move and you're dead men! Out, fellows, and put a rope on them!"

One of the spies, the weazen fellow, began to protest in excellent English:

"What do you mean by this? We haven't done anything to—." But Duncan snatched up a clump of grass roots and shoved it into the fellow's mouth. The other man cowered back and tried at first to keep his face away from the electric bull's-eye Clem threw on them. Through Duncan's dexterity with strong twine taken from Don's toolbox, both men had their arms tied behind them in a jiffy so that they winced with the pain.

"Do you fellows think this is funny? Let us loose, at once! We have no time for jokes!" demanded the taller one, gazing at Don's revolver in a manner that showed he knew it was no joke.

"But you had time to play one of your kind of jokes on that poor wounded soldier up on the hill," Clem returned and the thin face of the spy grew ghastly white. "We haven't been up on the hill," he asserted— but another wad of grass-roots stopped his talk also. Don took the bull's-eye from Clem and threw it into the tall man's face.

"Well, Stapley, I guess you know him; don't you?"

"The fellow on the train, sure enough," Clem said.

"Wonderful!" said Don. "You do have a lucid flash now and then." But before Clem could reply Don began to enlighten the spy:

"I guess you remember us back there in America. We got off at Lofton, too. We got your cronies, Shultz and the whiskered chap, and I got your pard up near Montdidier."

Of course the man could make no reply. Don continued:

"Duncan, you can run my car, I guess. You take these nice chaps into camp. In about half an hour they'll face a firing squad."

But Duncan shook his head. "What's in me has got to come out. I'm an ambulance driver and working to save people—ours and theirs, too—but that don't say I don't just love gettin' square more'n anything else on this green earth! I told the corporal here I have a little Indian in me. I have a heap and it's reached high mark right now. It might get the corporal in trouble and it may get me in trouble, but I reckon you're out of it, Richards. No matter; what I want is to be the firing squad that fixes these blood-smeared polecats. But I don't want to do it with a gun. You just leave it to me. I'm goin' to take 'em over here in this field an' stick a knife into—"

"No, Duncan, you are not going to do anything of the kind!" Don said in horror. "I won't consent to this being anything irregular. You may go along and see them shot, if you want to, but you can't knife them. Hold on there! Put that knife up, or I'm going to shoot it out of your fingers. It would just about break my heart to hurt you, old man, because I know you're good

14

stuff, but don't try that thing. Come, you've got more white blood in you than Indian and don't imitate these Huns."

Duncan stood looking earnestly at Don while he spoke. Then, without a word, he put his long-bladed claspknife into his pocket.

"You take my car, because it's surer than this one, and get these chaps where they'll do no more harm. I'll run their car and I'll have them send out for yours and fix it. I hope they'll let you get into the squad that does the shooting."

"I don't like to deprive you of your own car," Duncan said. It was easy to see that the fellow was true-blue, even if an act of savagery made his blood boil with desire for personal revenge.

"Your errand is more important than mine," Don continued. Besides, I'm glad, for Stapley and I would be sure to scrap on the way. I'd have to rub it in about his letting these men get away on the hill. And Stapley can't take anything from me good-naturedly. He can explain to you later what he thinks of me. I know already and I don't care a hoot. Come, Wash, climb out of there! We've got to see if we can make this ramshackle ambulance travel. So long, Duncan."

The military court gave the spies short
shift. Duncan was one of the firing squad
that did quick executions. The army *ambulancier* then went his way. Before morning
he was again driving his own ambulance
and Don Richards' car had been turned over
to him and the grinning Wash. Work on
Hill 165 had been finished.

"The marines are going to try to take
Bouresches and Belleau Wood to-day, I
hear," Don said to Duncan, as they met on
the road.

"I wish I was in that bunch of real men,"
Duncan replied and passed on. That was
the last Don ever saw of the brave fellow,
for Duncan was shifted north of the Oise
River where another Hun drive seemed immi-
nent, as they were short of ambulances
in that sector.

Don's orders were to run in close to the
American fighting forces without too grave
risk, and if there was an advance, to keep
pretty near to it, as there would necessarily
be many casualties. As the Germans had
learned already to recognize the Yanks as
their most formidable foes, they were sending
some of their best troops to stop them.

The Red Cross was showing splendid efficiency now. From stretcher bearers to dressing stations, from its own evacuation hospitals to ideally equipped bases and convalescent camps, it was the model for all things humane in warfare. Eager were its men and women in doing their share of the arduous and dangerous work, and proud, indeed, those who were identified in any way with its glorious efforts.

"Drive the enemy from Bouresches and Belleau Wood!" was the order from headquarters. Again, as one man, the marines went forward. The Huns must be taught that their advance at the Château-Thierry front was at an end.

"Pound the enemy's lines in Bouresches!" came the order to the artillery as a forerunner of the charge of the marines, and the artillery pounded. Across the grain and flowering fields marched the soldiers, advancing in thin lines, one after the other, the marines in the center and on either flank a battalion of doughboys, regulars of the United States army. This was the good old training in American fighting methods: Advance on a run and lie down, advance and lie down, the front rank shooting all the while, and when these fellows, who must bear the brunt